The Complete Guide to Trapping, Second Edition

by Brian P. Lawler

1936122

Hayden
Books

The Complete Guide to Trapping, Second Edition

Library of Congress Catalog Number: 94-075941
ISBN: 1-56830-098-0

97   96   95   4   3   2   1

Interpretation of the printing code: the rightmost double-digit number is the year of the book's printing; the rightmost single-digit number is the number of the book's printing. For example, a printing code of 95-1 shows that the first printing of the book occurred in 1995.

This book was produced digitally by Macmillan Computer Publishing and manufactured using 100% computer-to-plate technology (filmless process), by Shepard Poorman Communications Corporation, Indianapolis, Indiana.

Trademark Acknowledgments

Acknowledgments

Thanks to readers and editors Robert Hu of A&a Printers & Lithographers of Menlo Park, California; Kevin Nathanson, Director, PostScript Services, a division of W.E. Andrews Co., Bedford, Mass.; and Hans Hartman. Thanks to Walter Schild of Alan Lithograph, Professors Steve Mott and Phil Ruggles of Cal Poly, San Luis Obispo, California; and to John McWade, Publisher and Creative Director, *Before & After,* for their valuable input.

Thanks also to Thad McIlroy, Margene Filson, and other contributors from The Color Resource.

THE HAYDEN BOOKS TEAM

Publisher
Don Fowley

Editor-in-Chief
Michael Nolan

Acquisitions Editor
Robin Graham

Development Editor
Rebecca Tapley

Technical Editors
Stephen Graham
Gene Pemberton

Interior Designer
Paula Carroll

Cover Designer
Jay Corpus

Manufacturing Coordinator
Paul Gilchrist

Production Manager
Kelly Dobbs

Production Team Supervisor
Laurie Casey

Layout Technician
Rich Evers

Production Team
Dan Caparo, Kim Cofer,
Erika Millen, Regina Rexrode,
Christine Tyner, Karen Walsh

Indexer
Bront Davis

To Our Readers

You can reach Hayden Books with your comments and book ideas at the following:

Hayden Books
201 West 103rd Street
Indianapolis, IN 46290
800/428-5331 voice
800/448-3804 fax

E-mail addresses:

America Online: Hayden Bks
AppleLink: hayden.bks
CompuServe: 76350,3014
Internet: hayden@hayden.com

About the Author

Brian Lawler is a consultant and lecturer in the graphic arts industry. A graduate of the Cal Poly (San Luis Obispo, California) Graphic Communication program, he occasionally teaches at his alma mater.

As a student, he was production manager for Cal Poly's student-printed daily paper, curator of its printing museum, and president of the student printing club Mat Pica Pi.

He is a well-known speaker at regional and national trade shows and printing industry seminars, and lectures regularly to the graphic arts and photographic trades.

In 1973, Mr. Lawler founded Tintype Graphic Arts in San Luis Obispo, California. Tintype began as a design and typography firm, and later blossomed to include a photographic studio, a PostScript service bureau, conventional film assembly and complete prepress services.

His firm later merged with Blake Printing & Publishing, Inc., a commercial printing firm, and Lawler became an officer of that corporation, operating Tintype and making purchase decisions on high-tech equipment for the corporation. The equipment list included automated step-and-repeat equipment and a Crosfield scanner with electronic retouching equipment.

Lawler founded Tintype Tech, an innovative training facility within his firm for teaching desktop publishing skills to his customers. An Apple Training Alliance affiliate firm, *Tintype Tech* was run as a full-time adult school offering computer courses not only in graphic arts subjects but in business and computer science subjects as well.

His experience in preparing artwork for printing began with hand-set type and hot-metal linecasting machines; he knows the true meaning of etaoin/shrdlu.

He is a columnist with *Pre–* and a regular contributor to *MacUSER* magazine, and has several books in print including this book, *Inside Photo CD,* and *Photo CD Revealed.* He also was editor for over five years of *Ballooning,* an international magazine for sport balloonists.

For the past few years, Mr. Lawler has been touring the world lecturing the graphic arts industry in programs sponsored by Apple Computer, Leaf Systems, Radius, and Eastman Kodak Company.

Contents

Foreword

Introduction

1   **Basic Terms and Definitions**   6

2   **Conventional Lithographic Trapping**   12

3   **Why Do We Need Trapping?**   26

4   **How to Avoid Trapping**   36

5   **Special Trapping Situations**   44

6   **Trapping on the Desktop**   54

7   **Working with Dedicated Trapping Software**   72

8   **The State of the Art of Trapping**   86

9   **Workflow Considerations**   94

    Appendix A   The Color Resource Guide to Trapping   98

    Appendix B   Vendor List   128

    Appendix C   Bibliography   134

    Glossary   138

    Index   151

Foreword

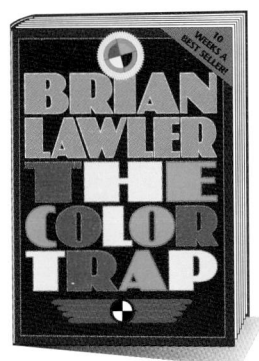

In the first edition of this book, I jokingly referred to my book becoming a bestseller. It's interesting that it turned out to be a bestseller in a specialized book market. Trapping is such an important and misunderstood topic that this book has become extraordinarily popular with graphic artists, printers, prepress specialists, and colleges and universities. It's very flattering to enjoy such success.

I could have written a spy novel ("Ten Weeks on the New York Times Bestseller List!!" foil-stamped on the cover), but somehow my training didn't lead to that.

I spent seven years in college acquiring a four-year degree in Graphic Communication ("We used to call it printing!"). Somewhere in that span of years I vaguely remember an instructor talking about trapping and the photographic processes involved in making multiple colors of ink print properly on a press despite the tiny shifts and irregularities in the movement of paper as it passes through these machines.

I regret that I don't remember which instructor it was, and I regret that it didn't make a stronger impression on me. I was on a career track that didn't include—in my perspective at the time—assembling film on a light table.

I got my diploma, and I started a graphic arts business—in the opposite order— and I did well. Over the years in business I learned a great deal about color separations, color trapping, and lithographic image assembly ("We used to call it stripping!").

Now, years later, I have become an expert in electronic prepress, instructing others in the details of film preparation using a computer instead of, or in addition to, a light table.

Although no bullets fly in this book, no one is taken hostage, and no clandestine activities take place in the dark of night, the book does unravel some mysteries of color printing, and I hope that what is contained in this book is useful to all who read it.

I still plan to write that spy novel—it'll be called *The Color Trap*. I hope that it, too, will be a bestseller.

Brian P. Lawler
San Luis Obispo, California
November, 1995

Introduction

In recent history, the electronic prepress industry has been beset by a number of technology-driven changes. First there was concern over imagesetters generating inaccurate film; then desktop designers wondered if type fonts were available in sufficient number to make the transition from conventional typesetting techniques. Now, color screen techniques are preoccupying designers and publishers—hence the need for more, easily digestible information on trapping.

Trapping color is a much more complicated issue than, for example, hyphenation and kerning, which can be solved with relative ease. Trapping demands the understanding and application of arcane or even secret principles to everyday art preparation. Everybody involved in the production of film for printing wishes there were an option called Trap readily available in the Print dialog box of every desktop publishing program. Then quality trapping could be accomplished with a single click of the mouse.

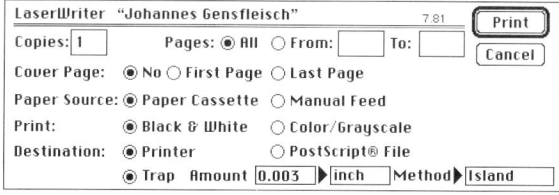

Fortunately, most popular page layout and illustration programs now boast automatic or semi-automatic trapping functions. There are even major-league products available on the market that trap entire documents as part of prepress production—a vast improvement over traditional trapping, but still not enough to remove the need for human participation.

So with trapping decisions falling more and more often to the designer, even though *they* won't do the trapping themselves, it is extremely important they make sure that *someone* does it and does it well.

Why a book about trapping?

The subject of trapping has been relegated to the back pages of trade school textbooks for too long. In this book, I intend to make up for these deficiencies and provide readers with a full explanation of trapping, from the definition of the problem to the description of various problem-solving methods using both conventional photographic methods and electronic techniques via the computer.

This book is not a step-by-step handbook about how to make traps using a contact frame and duplicating film. What you *will* find here is an explanation of the process of trapping—when to trap, what color to use, and how much to trap. This will help the reader understand what causes register problems, how trapping can compensate for most of these problems, and how electronic trapping makes creating traps easier and more efficient.

By focusing on the challenge of preparing artwork correctly in order to achieve excellent printing, this book will endure in the face of ceaseless change in the computer graphics world.

How this book is organized

Each of the nine chapters in this book addresses a specific aspect of the trapping puzzle. Readers who are already familiar with the background of trapping should feel free to jump ahead to the more technical information, but newcomers to this subject may prefer to study each chapter in detail.

Chapter 1, "Basic Terms and Definitions," introduces the rudimentary vocabulary of color trapping, including all the (seemingly) ninety-nine names for the trapping process.

Chapter 2, "Conventional Lithographic Trapping," explains each step of the traditional trapping process in detail, along with a consideration of such issues as spreads, chokes, standards, and more.

Chapter 3, "Why Do We Need Trapping?," distinguishes between which components of a design should be trapped and which should not, as well as the reasons why trapping is necessary after all.

Chapter 4, "How to Avoid Trapping," offers some suggestions on how to get around the tricky trapping process—and when it's a good idea to let someone else do the dirty work.

Chapter 5, "Special Trapping Situations," examines particular examples that bring on the challenge of trapping, such as trapping backgrounds and text, photos, and gradations.

Chapter 6, "Trapping on the Desktop," takes a look at desktop trapping capabilities in popular programs such as Adobe Photoshop, Macromedia FreeHand, QuarkXPress, and Adobe PageMaker.

Chapter 7, "Working with Dedicated Trapping Software," discusses the benefits of using trapping software products like Adobe TrapWise and IslandTrapper.

Chapter 8, "The State of the Art of Trapping," discusses the recent changes in graphic arts technologies and procedures, and what needs to be done to ensure quality trapping takes place now that roles and responsibilities are shifting.

Chapter 9, "Workflow Considerations," can help establish priorities when considering all the options for trapping and the different responsibilities of all the professionals involved in the prepress process.

At the back of the book, a glossary and index are provided to help you reference whichever particular area or subject within trapping you want. Additionally, the three appendixes present you with additional resources for information on trapping: Appendix A, "The Color Resource Guide to Trapping," deals with trapping in Adobe Illustrator, Macromedia FreeHand, QuarkXPress, Adobe PageMaker, and Adobe Photoshop. Appendix B provides contact information on trapping software and hardware vendors, and Appendix C lists bibliographic resources for more reading on trapping color.

The disk tucked in the plastic sleeve on the inside back cover contains the The Color Resource Trapping Tutorial, an interactive multimedia presentation that covers the basics of trapping color in simple, easy-to-understand terminology.

Who this book is for

The Complete Guide to Trapping, Second Edition is written primarily for graphic designers and publishers involved in document production, but it also applies to the work of printers, prepress specialists, and service bureau operators. I have assumed that the reader, therefore, is familiar with desktop publishing hardware and software, possesses basic working knowledge of Macintosh and/or PC computers, and has some experience with the printing process.

It's also a basic assumption that the reader has been frustrated with the difficulty of using popular desktop publishing and illustration software programs to do trapping. The information in this book is designed to be clear and valuable to readers of all experience levels, but if you want more information on application-specific techniques, consult the user manuals that came with the particular program you're using.

1 Basic Terms and Definitions

WHAT IS TRAPPING?

TRAPPING BY OTHER NAMES

WHEN TRAPPING IS *NOT* TRAPPING

REGISTER

WHAT IS TRAPPING?

Trapping is the intentional overlap of colors in a printed project that prevents inevitable printing errors from showing. It is compensation—in advance of production—for the human and mechanical errors that result in misregistration of images on a printing press.

The images on the left are not trapped. Misregistration on the printing press, human error, and environmental factors all can contribute to the need for building traps to prevent register errors from showing. The images have been trapped—the intentional overlap of colors to prevent register error on-press. Trapping should not call undue attention to itself, yet it should be adequate to prevent unprinted paper from showing through the intersections of colors that are slightly out of register.

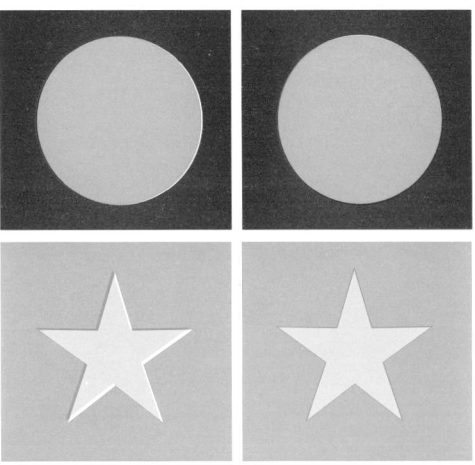

TRAPPING BY OTHER NAMES

Many people don't call this process trapping at all. They use terms like "spreads and chokes," "fatties and skinnies," "shrink and spread," "lap register," or "making grips" to describe the technique of *trapping* misregistration on the press.

Conventional printers, who may be new to the terminology of the electronic prepress industry, need to become aware of changing terms. While I was in the printing plant that produced the advance literature on this book, the foreman of the lithographic department said to me, "A book about trapping. It's about time!" He went on to tell me horror stories about trying to print customer-supplied film, and then he insisted that the correct term for trapping is "making grips." I smiled and assured him I would take his advice into account.

Regardless of what you call the technique, be sure to trap, for without correct trapping we cannot get excellent printing, and excellent printing is our objective.

WHEN TRAPPING IS *NOT* TRAPPING

There's another definition of trapping that engenders confusion about trapping color in the graphic arts industry. *Trapping, wet trapping,* and *dry trapping* are all terms used to describe the application of multiple layers of ink, the ability of each layer to adhere to previous layers of ink, and the interaction of those inks. Most graphic arts dictionaries list this general definition first (or exclusively), and only mention trapping (as the intentional overlapping of colors) as a footnote.

Dry trapping is used by printers and press operators to describe the adhesion of one coat of ink over another that's already dry. If the base ink is not formulated correctly, the overprinted ink will not adhere correctly. The tack (adhesion) of ink is measured with a device called an inkometer.

Wet trapping describes how overprinted inks adhere to and contaminate each other when printed wet-on-wet. Inks must be formulated and printed in the correct order to trap correctly. If a layer is too thick, or the formulation of ink vehicle and pigments is wrong, the top layers adhere incorrectly to those already set down, and a color shift can result.

While wet and dry trapping are serious concerns, they are purely ink-on-paper problems, and not under the direct control of designers and publishers. We will concentrate on the type of trapping designers and desktop publishers can control.

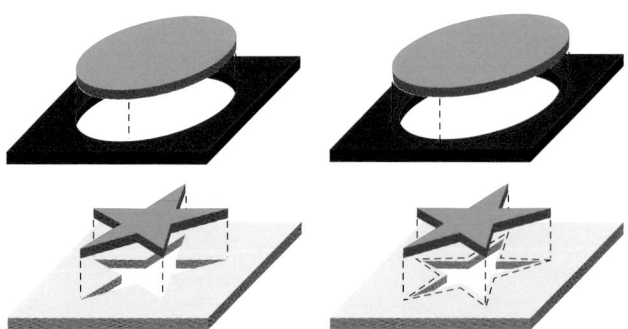

Register error, or misregistration, *can be overcome by building traps into artwork. The illustrations on the left show untrapped artwork, while those on the right demonstrate how trapping creates art with intentionally overlapping colors.*

REGISTER

In the context of trapping, *register* (also known as *fit)* is the accurate positioning of two or more colors or tints of ink on separate pieces of film. The Graphic Arts Technical Foundation (GATF) uses three terms to define the difficulty of printing a job: hairline register (often called tight register), loose register, and lap register.

Hairline register requires colors to abut, or match boundaries, with no unprinted paper showing through, and no intentional overlapping of colors (or, with no trapping). When a job is designed with loose register, colored objects are spaced far enough apart that register problems will not be easily visible. In other words, the objects have enough open space between them, a little more or less space will not be noticeable. Lap register jobs have built-in register compensation (or, trapping), making them easier to keep in register on press. This is the most common kind of register used in commercial printing, but the cost of preparing the overlapping traps is significant, and estimators must plan on having their prepress staff build traps into the job, whether those traps are created photomechanically or electronically.

You might assume that everything would be easier if you just paid the higher price of printing in hairline register, and forgot about trapping. It's not that easy. A broad range of mechanical, environmental, and human factors combine to make it impossible to keep printing in absolute register (described in detail in Chapter 3). This is the simple reason for the existence of color trapping—to compensate as best as possible for these inevitable printing problems.

Most graphic design and page layout programs default to "knockout" colors from one another. The result is an unprinted hole in the surrounding color that is exactly the size of the second color. This is the very condition that creates the potential for misregistration on the printing press and the situation addressed by trapping.

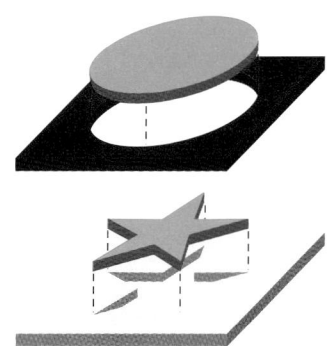

For a complete alphabetical listing of terms and definitions, consult the Glossary on page 138.

2 Conventional Lithographic Trapping

SPREADS AND CHOKES

EXPOSURE TO DUPLICATING FILM FOR A SPREAD

PHOTOGRAPHIC TRAPPING AND IMAGE QUALITY

HOW MUCH TO TRAP IMAGES

VARYING STANDARDS IN PRINTING PLANTS

HOW COLORS SHOULD TRAP

WHICH COLOR IS DARKER?

TRAPPING WITH TINTS

PRINTING WITH SPOT COLORS

THE THORNY ISSUES OF TRAPPING

In this chapter, we will explore conventional lithographic techniques: how traps are created by the overexposure of film to create spreads and chokes. At first glance, this information may seem unnecessary (if not the makings of dry reading) given the increasing capabilities of electronic prepress techniques, but understanding traditional trapping methods will help give you a grasp of the entire trapping picture. If you're still unconvinced, the essential techniques for trapping in electronic prepress are discussed in Chapter 7, "Working with Dedicated Trapping Software."

SPREADS AND CHOKES

Conventional lithographers produce trapping films by a system of gross overexposure onto either contact film for chokes, or duplicating film for spreads. When two different colors meet in a printing job, it is common for one of the two to be *spread* into the other: the film is overexposed to cause a fattening of the image area. (The result of this overexposure is also called a *spread*.) Conventional photographic trapping requires that a spread negative be created from the original, by contact exposure through a stack of film layers in a sandwich.

Choking requires a conceptual shift. Instead of enlarging the foreground object (as is done in a spread) the background color is enlarged, which effectively chokes the image being trapped with an overlap of the background color. The foreground object retains its dimension, but its outline is reduced inward by an overlap from the background color. To make a choke photographically, negative-acting (also called contact) film is used in the same sandwich arrangement. The result is a film with an area that has been reduced because of this diffused-light overexposure. Usually these choked films are a reverse of what they need to be (positive), so another generation contact is made to reverse the image back to a usable piece of film.

Note

Both spreading and choking jobs may result in changes in the overall design of the print job, since color is shifted or expanded into other colored areas and the resulting blend may not have been part of the original design concept.

This simplified explanation of such techniques may give the wrong impression about the consensus—and the consequences—of using different trapping solutions. In one plant I visited in preparation for writing this book, there were 12 artist-lithographers on staff who described twelve different trapping techniques when I polled them. It was painfully obvious that no standards had been established in their plant for the production of trapped film. What mattered more in their facility was that the film was being trapped, and that was good enough.

After some testing and education, all the lithographers were taught to make film traps the same way. Exposures and diffusion thicknesses were posted in the contacting area of the plant, and consistency was finally reached.

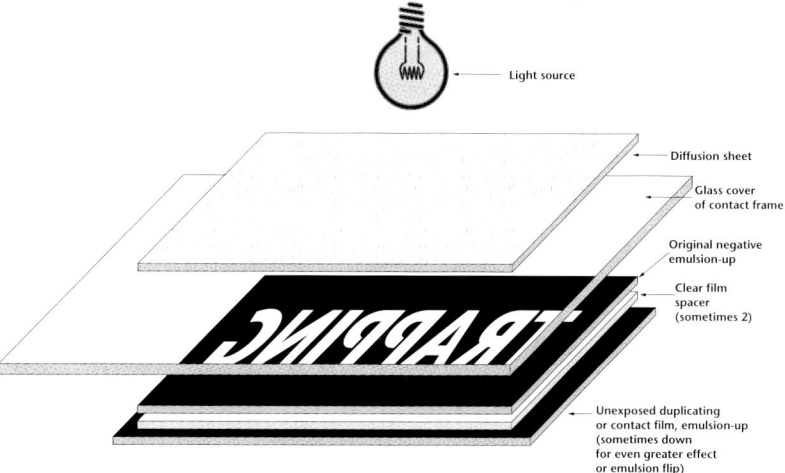

The sandwich of films needed to make a choke or spread exposure consists of the original line negative (or positive), a clear film layer, and an unexposed sheet of film on the bottom. Modern-day lithographers are using films that can be handled in "bright light" conditions, making the process possible under yellow fluorescent lighting. The exposure of the sandwich is usually made through a diffusion sheet, creating scattered light and a more reliable spread pattern. By controlling the thickness of the sandwich and the exposure, relatively accurate spreads can be made with consistency.

While many techniques exist for choking and spreading images photographically, they all follow the same basic steps:

1. Contacting in a vacuum frame through a sandwich of films

2. Overexposure

3. Light diffusion during exposure

The combination of sandwiching films and the overexposure of the resulting film creates the spread or choke. Because contacting films are high-contrast by nature, the overexposure serves to enhance the spread; otherwise overexposure has no deleterious effect on the image. Where controls exist, it is the exposure through the sandwich that results in the spread or choke. Exposure values for spreading and choking are typically three to five times normal.

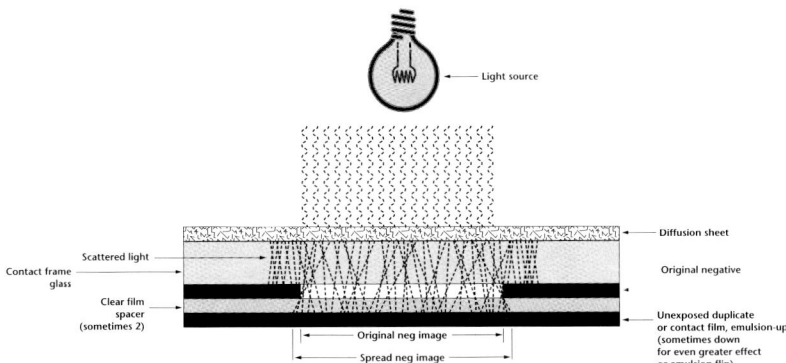

A cross-section view of a conventional spread exposure shows the light source followed by the diffusion sheet. Scattered light passes through the original, then through the spacer film(s) and finally hits the unexposed film on the bottom of the stack. By that time, the image is spread significantly compared to the original.

Exposure to duplicating film for a spread

A lithographer exposes a negative through a sheet (or a stack of sheets) of clear film in a contact frame under vacuum pressure. On the bottom of the stack is a fresh (unexposed) piece of duplicating film. The emulsions of the original and the new film face the same direction (either up or down, it makes no difference) in the sandwich.

The sandwich of films is exposed to light, which is scattered by a diffusion sheet. The clear films in the middle of the sandwich allow light to scatter around the edges of the image, exposing more than the original area. After processing, a spread film is delivered.

One or two sheets of clear film will usually suffice for these sandwiches. Typical lithographic film is 0.003 or 0.004 of an inch thick, so two sheets will build a gap of 0.006 or 0.008 of an inch for the diffused light to pass through. The value of the resulting spread is controlled by exposure. More exposure results in more spread.

The creation of correct spreads requires the diffusion of light during exposure. To accomplish this, the operator shakes a plastic diffusion sheet above the vacuum frame to produce randomly scattered light. Constant motion is required for spread value consistency. While some operators leave this diffusion step out, it can result in inconsistent spread or choke thickness.

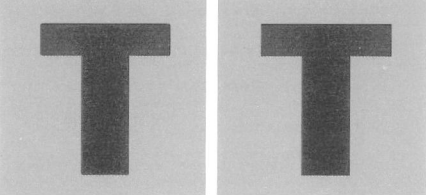

Conventional photographic trapping techniques, left, round-off the sharp edges of images, leaving them slightly damaged in the process. Most electronic trapping techniques, by contrast, will not damage the sharpness of an image, as demonstrated by the letter on the right.

Photographic trapping and image quality

Photographic trapping has a number of inherent flaws. Among them is the degradation of image sharpness that occurs when a film is spread by excessive exposure from diffused light. Straying from the otherwise razor-sharp quality of process camera film and emulsion-to-emulsion contacts, film that has been spread is soft on the edges as a result of having been created by off-contact exposure and diffused light.

In photographic choke-and-spread work, sharp corners of any image get rounded off. The electronic variation of the process is much more precise. PostScript lines maintain their thickness, all corners remain sharp, and the process is repeatable and thus more controllable.

HOW MUCH TO TRAP IMAGES

To determine how much trapping is necessary, ask your printer how much trap is appropriate for his or her equipment. Most sheet-fed offset presses require 0.003 of an inch of trap, while some web presses, especially newspaper presses, require a bit more.

Method of printing	Substrate	Halftone frequency	Trap (in.)	Trap (mm.)	Trap (pt.)*
Sheet-fed offset	Gloss coated	150 lpi 60 d/cm.	.003 in.	.08 mm.	.25 pt.
Sheet-fed offset	Uncoated	150 lpi 60 d/cm.	.003 in.	.08 mm.	.25 pt.
Web-fed offset	Gloss coated	150 lpi 60 d/cm.	.004 in.	.10 mm.	.30 pt.
Web-fed offset	Uncoated commercial	133 lpi 52 d/cm.	.005 in.	.13 mm.	.40 pt.
Web-fed offset	Newsprint	100 lpi 40 d/cm.	.006 in.	.15 mm.	.45 pt.
Flexography	Coated	133 lpi 52 d/cm.	.006 in.	.15 mm.	.45 pt.
Flexography	Newsprint	100 lpi 40 d/cm.	.008 in.	.20 mm.	.60 pt.
Flexography	Kraft (corrugated, other)	65 lpi 25 d/cm.	.010 in.	.25 mm.	.75 pt.
Screen printing (wet-on-wet)	Fabric	any	0	0	0
Screen printing (dried)	Paper, fabric, other	100 lpi 40 d/cm.	.006 in.	.15 mm.	.45 pt.
Gravure	Gloss coated	150 lpi 60 d/cm.	.003 in.	.08 mm.	.25 pt.

*Point values are rounded for convenience of entry.

Sheet-fed presses are commonly used to produce high-quality printing on glossy papers in full color. This type of printing is usually printed by arranging dots in a frequency of 150 to 200 dots per inch, more commonly referred to as lines per inch. Thus, when printing 150 lines per inch, each line would be representing a row of dots with each halftone dot measuring 0.00667 of an inch in diameter (1÷150).

Newspapers use coarser halftones as a result of high absorptivity of the paper used and the speed of the presses. Newspaper press register is rarely as good as sheet-fed offset printing, thus extra trapping is required. An 85 lines per inch halftone is typical for newsprint, resulting in a recommended trapping amount of 0.006 of an inch.

Some presses and printing conditions require more or less trapping. Be sure to check with the printing firm doing the job to get its specification for trapping values.

Some printers will not be able to express trapping values in thousandths of an inch or in points. Ask in halftone dots—you'll get your answer.

Ask the following questions and perform the following calculations:

1. Determine the frequency halftone the printer usually uses.

2. Divide that number into 1 to get the decimal value of the dot.

3. Divide that number by 2 to get the trap needed.

For example: Printer A, when asked for a trap value, says, "About half of a dot." Your response should be, "What frequency halftone do you usually print?"

"Oh, we print 150-line halftones."

Your answer is at hand: 1 inch divided by 150 equals 0.00667 of an inch. Divide that by 2 (*half* of a dot) to get 0.0033—that's your trap.

VARYING STANDARDS IN PRINTING PLANTS

One of the great ironies of the trapping issue is that even in the most professional of lithographic shops, the technique will vary from one person to the next, even though lithographic foremen will swear that their techniques are rock-solid and consistent.

I asked a number of film assemblers in several different printing plants about chokes and spreads, and got a different answer from every one. This indicates an issue that must be addressed by all quality-driven firms: Control equals quality.

One film assembler I interviewed said, "I usually make my spreads by shaking a diffusion sheet over the top of the vacuum frame during the exposure."

"How much exposure do you use to produce a typical spread?" I asked.

"About twice the normal exposure, but sometimes as much as five times as much," he responded.

Further investigation revealed that he did not use the light integrator to get the correct exposure—*he guessed* by turning on the exposure lamp for a while, then turning it off again!

As a solution to the problems pointed out by his answers to my questions, his printing firm instituted a set of new policies:

- They established standard techniques for choke-and-spread exposures and posted them prominently in the lithographic preparation areas.

- They made certain that everyone used these techniques.

- If it was necessary to change any of the techniques, the new procedure was promptly posted.

Printing firms that invest in quality control at every step in the process will see higher productivity and better profitability. Failure to follow the path of quality control will result in haphazard products that are often rejected by the buyer.

HOW COLORS SHOULD TRAP

Dominant-subordinate relationships are the most common criteria for determining which color traps the other. In the simplest cases, the lighter color should be spread into the darker color. But it is sometimes difficult to determine which of two (or more) colors is lighter.

There is in fact a precise measure of lightness or darkness—the grayscale value of a color. The grayscale measures the overall luminosity or brightness of the image. If you convert a color image to grayscale in a program like Adobe Photoshop, the colors are changed into the corresponding grayscale value. In an RGB image, the luminosity is normally derived from this formula:

$$L = .3R + .59G + .11B$$

where L is luminosity, a sum of the products of the red, green and blue percentages multiplied by the factors given. The higher the luminosity value, the higher the grayscale equivalent or overall tonal value. But in spite of these absolute values, colors of similar luminosity (for example, browns and purples) can be very hard to distinguish.

When two colors of similar darkness meet, the decision as to which gets spread or choked is determined more by the content of the objects than by the colors. Text or other items that contain the detail in the image are usually left alone while the opposing color is spread into them. Because text is damaged most easily by trapping techniques, it is wise to remember the admonition to *leave text alone whenever possible*. Exceptions to this rule abound, but at least place this rule as a priority.

Different people will have different ideas about how colors should trap, and it is wise not to get involved in extensive arguments over such matters. If you follow the advice in the next section on dominant and subordinate colors, you'll go far. Your printer will appreciate getting film that has traps built in, and the job will come out fine. The worst case is that the colors of some of the traps will not be correct, but in all but the most extreme situations the only one who will notice this is you.

Which color is darker?

Using the color wheel illustrated here, it is possible to determine the relative brightness of any color compared to another. This color wheel parallels the color positions of the Apple Color Picker, which is selected from the Control Panel and from within many Macintosh applications.

Comparing two colors using this wheel is relatively simple. As you move toward the center of the wheel, colors will be more gray; at the absolute center is black. "Pure" primary and secondary colors are at the circumference of the wheel. By plotting any color along a spoke from the circumference toward the center, and comparing that to the plot of the second color, the darker color will be determined by the arrows around the outside of the circle.

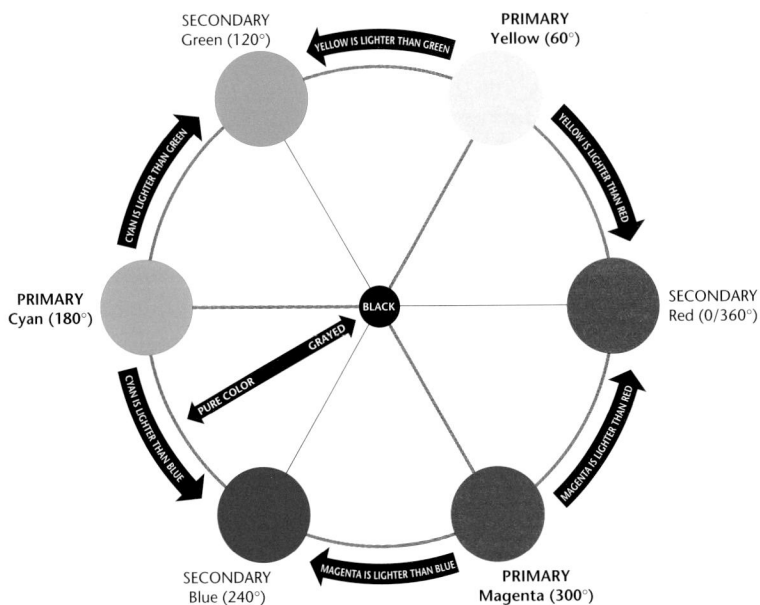

Colors can be found on this subtractive color wheel, and compared to another color. When analyzing the choice, hue is selected around the circumference of the wheel while value follows the spokes of the wheel. Darker colors are found toward the center, pure colors at the circumference. Determining the darker of two colors using this wheel is highly subjective, yet quite easy.

While this is perhaps overly simplistic, it is functional, and a reasonable visual reference for the average person making a dominant-subordinate color decision.

Trapping with tints

Another trapping method, which is seldom used in conventional film assembly, is trapping two colors with *a screen tint* of one of the two. This would be very difficult using conventional techniques because it requires the creation of a negative of just the trap line, an image that is only a few thousandths of an inch thick. Once that negative is created, a negative screen tint must be taped to its back, resulting in parts of halftone dots being printed in the trap line alone.

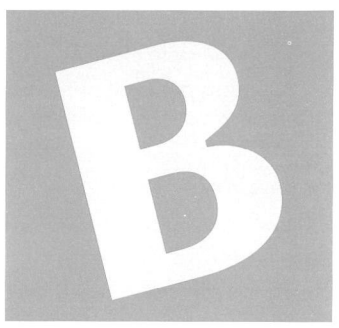

The trapping of the left illustration creates a bright green trap line (exaggerated here intentionally), while trapping with a tint creates a more pleasing result. The right-hand example uses a 20 percent tint of cyan for the trap line. Extraordinarily difficult in conventional lithography, the process is relatively simple using the electronic techniques now at our disposal. In many cases, a screen tint of a color is preferable to a solid color, preventing a new, more intense color from being created at the color intersections.

Alignment of the screen angle must be exact, or the resulting image could create an unsightly moiré pattern (an interference pattern created by screens that are close in frequency and angle to one another, yet not exactly the same). The process is too difficult and time-consuming to carry out with conventional contacting and film assembly techniques.

With electronic prepress, the option of trapping a yellow-cyan intersection with a 20 percent tint of cyan is quite simple. Compare a pale green trapping line with a bright green intersection between yellow and cyan colors, and you will see the advantage of using screen tints to accomplish trapping for these circumstances.

A tint of a color calls far less attention to itself than a solid trapping line does, and the result is a more attractive color intersection. The trap is less likely to stand out.

Because electronic trapping techniques allow for such screen tint traps to be created easily and accurately, it's wise to consider their use for some color intersections. New trapping software allows the user to define whether trapping takes place as a spread, a choke, or "both." When both are selected, this trap is technically being created with a common color going both ways.

These screened traps are particularly effective with pastel colors, and also are an excellent solution to many of our everyday trapping dilemmas.

Printing with spot colors

Spot colors and process colors of ink are all transparent, and unless some special ink formulation is being used, the order in which inks are printed should make no difference with regard to color trapping. Only when a job calls for metallic inks or secondary processes like screen printing or foil stamping do the considerations for trapping need to be changed according to the order in which the processes are performed.

These inks and foils are often opaque, and thus do not behave the way process and spot color inks do. Consult with the printer to get the correct information on trapping with opaque inks and foils.

THE THORNY ISSUES OF TRAPPING

Trapping theory often becomes impossible to reconcile when multiple lines of color cross a unique color background. What do you do? You review the options, then choose a color to spread, make the trap, and accept the consequences. Three experienced film assemblers might offer three unique solutions to this problem. When in doubt, ask your printer or a seasoned film assembler for advice. Their experience will present additional options.

3
Why Do We Need Trapping?

MISREGISTRATION: THE HEART OF THE MATTER

    BOUNCE

    PAPER STRETCH

    PAPER COMPOSITION AND MANUFACTURING

    PRESS WEAR

    MULTI-COLOR PRINTING ON SINGLE-COLOR PRESSES

    HUMAN ERROR IN FILM ASSEMBLY

    POOR QUALITY FILM AND/OR STRIPPING MATERIALS

PROBLEMS WITH PLATEMAKING AND FILM HANDLING EQUIPMENT

    LIGHT INTEGRATORS

    HUMAN ERROR IN PLATEMAKING

PRESS PROBLEMS

    POOR ENVIRONMENTAL CONTROLS

With so much helpful and time-saving design technology at our fingertips, the need for trapping—and the human attention good trapping requires—may seem obsolete. However, a major part of the problem of trapping is determining which components of the job should be trapped, and which should not. Once this determination is made, what objects are trapped and how the trap is made become equally important issues.

First, it is essential to understand the factors that contribute to misregistration—the problem that trapping solves. In this chapter and the next two to follow, we'll take a look at the reasons why problems occur and how they can be solved.

MISREGISTRATION: THE HEART OF THE MATTER

Misregistration—inaccuracies in the positioning of two or more colors on the printed sheet—results in unprinted paper peeking through an intersection of colors where no unprinted area was intended. Even the tiniest error in printing can be seen as a thin white line showing between colors on a sheet. The human eye can easily spot a line only 0.002 of an inch in thickness when that line has great enough contrast, and white (or unprinted) paper stands out well against solid colors printed over it.

In traditional prepress and printing work, the factors contributing to misregistration are

- Errors in film assembly

- Film or stripping material instability

- Errors in platemaking and film handling prior to platemaking

- Poorly maintained printing presses or poorly trained operators

- Paper inaccuracy or instability resulting in size change

- Lack of proper environmental controls

Each of these factors can cause misregistration on its own, though several factors typically "conspire" to cause misregistration.

Bounce

The most common problem causing misregistration on a sheet-fed printing press that is in otherwise good condition is bounce. When paper in a stack is raised into the feeding mechanism of a printing press, it's accelerated from a standstill to full-speed in a matter of microseconds. Also, at each unit in a multi-color printing press the paper frequently changes hands as one set of grippers passes each sheet on to the next. In the midst of this process, paper will occasionally bounce against a stop, or twist slightly in the gripper mechanism, causing a register error to occur between colors. Even a minute error can be visible—remember, the human eye can see gaps as small as .002 of an inch.

Paper stretch

Paper is subjected to severe physical stress in the process of printing. By the time it has finished its trip through the machine, it has been subjected to extreme pressure and exposed to moisture and to heat.

As one set of grippers hands a sheet to the next, each set pulls harder on one side of the sheet than the other, and something has to give. If presses are allowed to get out of adjustment or allowed to wear excessively, the stretching effect on paper can be serious and irreparable misregistrations can occur.

Paper composition and manufacturing

Sometimes the paper itself can be the cause of some register problems. Poor quality paper or lighter stocks that tend to wave and flare can contribute to misregistration, but often it's rooted in the manufacturing process. Paper mills create paper in huge rolls, then slit the rolls into smaller widths and re-roll or sheet the paper for shipment. In some mills, paper is slit, interleaved, then sheeted. Occasionally this interleaving of sheets from opposite sides of a master roll results in press problems.

Paper mills also deliver paper that has inconsistent slitting, making the edge of the sheet—critical for precise register—vary from sheet to sheet. If a press operator is not watching closely for this kind of problem, register errors can occur. When the edges of sheets are so inconsistent that they begin to cause press register problems, the operator has no choice but to remove the stock from the press, and have it trimmed along one edge in a guillotine paper cutter for a more accurate register edge. (In fact this paper problem is so common that many printers pre-trim all stock used for multi-color printing, a costly investment in quality assurance.)

A California printer once found that *every other sheet* in a stack was of a different caliper! The press packing (the adjustment for overall impression) was thus wrong for half the job resultinged in two different printing jobs being performed in one pass.

When the printer discovered the problem, his only recourse was to hand sort the sheets, piling every other sheet onto a different stack, and then printing the job as two runs using different press packing for each run.

Press wear

As presses get older, they cannot hold the tight tolerances they once held and register problems start to creep into production. As a result, trapping must be built into every job to prevent the wear from showing in all the final printed products. The only solution to these problems, of course, is to purchase new equipment—keeping in mind that higher quality presses last longer than less expensive and lesser quality machines.

Multi-color printing on single-color presses

All of the press problems mentioned are made worse when printing multi-color jobs on a single-color printing press over a period of shifts or days. Lifts of paper (small stacks of printed sheets) allowed to rest for drying during the changeover from one color to the next can change dramatically, making subsequent register more difficult. Register problems become more acute as a result of paper changing size while drying or after being exposed to moisture on the press.

Under these circumstances, the best course of action is to reduce environmental change to a minimum, and to allow the printed sheets to rest for the shortest possible time between color runs.

Similar problems can also occur on two-color presses used for four-color printing, so use the same procedures to ward off misregistration.

Human error in film assembly

In conventional prepress work, trapping problems don't often result from human error—most are purely mechanical. Human miscalculations begin to show up as jobs become more complex and require more personal, individual attention on the part of the printer.

All it takes for a register error to start in film assembly is for one piece of film to be positioned and taped out of register relative to the other films in the job. If proofs are not made, or if errors are not caught in proofing, this register error will go all the way to press.

Poor quality film and/or stripping materials

Few printers will admit that less expensive materials are sometimes substituted for the real thing, since price is usually the bottom line—why spend $1.00 per square foot for stable clear film when $0.15 acetate *appears* to be the same?

The reason for investing in quality material may not show up until the press is running, when an image slips out of register because the film changed size. How does that $0.85 savings stand up against $500 per hour press downtime? All things considered, not very well.

A printer in Minnesota had an opportunity to buy a bulk of plain acetate plastic sheeting for his lithographic prep department. He got a great deal on the materials at about one-third the cost of the polyester plastic films he was using in production.

Minnesota is a place where the humidity changes rapidly and drastically. As the weather changed, so did the size of these carrier sheets. When summer arrived, the humidity soared to near-rain intensity and the inexpensive acetate sheets grew by almost one-eighth of an inch in one direction and about half that much in the other direction. Some jobs that had been assembled on a mix of stable polyester films and plain acetate were so far out of register that they needed restripping to correct the problem.

Because the materials looked the same, and were used in combination with the good film, the problem of shrinking and stretching film was impossible to detect by examination. The staff had to wait until something went out of register to determine which jobs to re-strip, adding considerable additional cost.

PROBLEMS WITH PLATEMAKING AND FILM HANDLING EQUIPMENT

Most printers invest heavily in the best presses, cutters, and bindery equipment they can afford because they know the payoff is worth the expense. Some printers, however, skimp on exposure measurement equipment even though mediocre vacuum pumps, exposure frames, and exposure systems all have an effect on quality and consistency.

In order to maintain near-perfect quality, the printer must have precision vacuum exposure frames, light integrators for exposure consistency, and processing machines to ensure that the plates made tomorrow will match those made today. The printer must also have the right tools for measuring (and thus controlling) quality—densitometers, micrometers, packing gauges. They must all be of good quality, well maintained, and regularly cleaned.

Vacuum contact should be measured often for consistency. The technique used by film assemblers and platemakers for laying film on top of film for duplication and exposure should also be consistent. With even one person using a different technique for handling film in the exposure frame, register control can go out the window, so take the whole printing process into consideration when looking for ways to reduce errors.

Light integrators

Timers are fine for timing bread in the oven, but light integrators are also essential when it comes to producing quality film and plate exposure. Even if it's measured and regulated accurately, time is not a good measure of exposure.

Standard electrical feeds can have wide variability in voltage, and unless power conditioning equipment is installed, there can be significant lamp brightness variation. To compensate for this variation, light integrator units measure photons of light hitting a sensor at the film plane, and adjust the exposure unit to give the plate or film consistent exposure, time after time.

Light integrators also compensate for the long-term lamp decay in exposure systems. A metal halide lamp, which decays slowly over a ten-month period, does not give any indication of that decay to its human operators. A light integrator will still count its photons and adjust exposure accordingly.

Human error in platemaking

Most printers employ well-trained people for plate exposure—it's too great an economic risk to hire cheap labor for such an important part of the printing job. Yet human error is the greatest factor contributing to register problems that result from poor platemaking.

While it seems that platemaking is a low cost area of the printing plant, further down the production line the high-cost press area is waiting for good printable plates. A Heidelberg 40-inch five-color press costs about $500 per hour to sit on a printer's floor during an eight-hour shift. If that press sits idle because of poor quality plates, the cost of the platemaking department *increases* by another $500 per hour. Suddenly quality platemaking becomes extraordinarily important—and more expensive.

A large North Carolina printer had a severe problem holding register on the outer trailing edges of eight-page signatures. The press foreman had his operators stretching the plates, attempting to get them to register from color to color. It didn't solve the problem, so they returned for new plates time and time again.

Sometimes these new plates worked perfectly; sometimes they duplicated the original problem in a new spot. By keeping good records of his press problems, the foreman determined that plates made by a single person were consistently acceptable, while plates made by two people, on two exposure frames, were causing the problem—each platemaker had a different technique for squeezing the air out of film when laid over the plate. One fellow wiped the air out in three straight passes, while another used a center-out sweeping technique, and a third swept from left to the right. When *any two* of these platemakers made plates for one job, the plates wouldn't fit!

The company established two new policies: First, only one platemaker could make all colors of a single job; and second, all platemakers had to use the same technique for squeezing air out of film.

Fortunately, careful trapping can compensate for some platemaking problems. Sometimes the error is too great, and in these cases new plates must be made.

PRESS PROBLEMS

In a perfect world, paper would pass straight through a printing press, it would accept ink in the right amounts, and it would never move, stretch, or distort in any way.

In reality, paper is a highly pliable medium and presses are only so accurate. As the paper runs from feeder to delivery unit through one, two, three, four (or more) sets of high-pressure rollers—subjected to tension, extreme heat, water, ink, and mechanical inconsistencies—the ink often gets misplaced, causing misregistration.

The press itself is most often the problem, but operator experience is also a big factor as is attention to detail. Senior press operators have fewer problems than trainees, and newer presses print with fewer register problems than older models.

Some printing companies have low standards of quality, or they push for greater output than a crew and machine can deliver while maintaining high quality.

Each of these press problems can cause misregistration that trapping can, in most cases, overcome.

Poor environmental controls

Air conditioning and heating, as well as air filtration and humidity control, are significant factors in maintaining quality in the film preparation and press departments of any printing company. In the short run, savings on air conditioning equipment may seem attractive, but ultimately they return in the long run in the form of film problems, printing press difficulties, paper shrinkage, or stretch. The savings are quickly lost in the cost of downtime.

A medium-size printer outside of Boise, Idaho, had significant press problems relating to humidity. Paper was unstable in the dry winter weather. As a result, warehousing time was increased to let the paper adjust to local humidity (money was spent on paper just sitting in the warehouse), deadlines were missed, jobs were spoiled, and the cost of doing business rose. The firm's problems with the weather seemed insurmountable.

Finally the production manager suggested a major investment in humidification equipment, which the company installed. Vaporizing over 35 gallons of water into the heating and ventilation system per shift caused the problems the company had with printing papers virtually to disappear.

4

How to Avoid Trapping

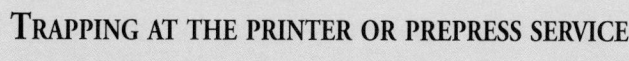

TRAPPING AT THE PRINTER OR PREPRESS SERVICE

DOING IT YOURSELF

OVERPRINTING: NO KNOCKOUT, NO TRAPPING

"NATURAL" TRAPPING: COMMON COLORS

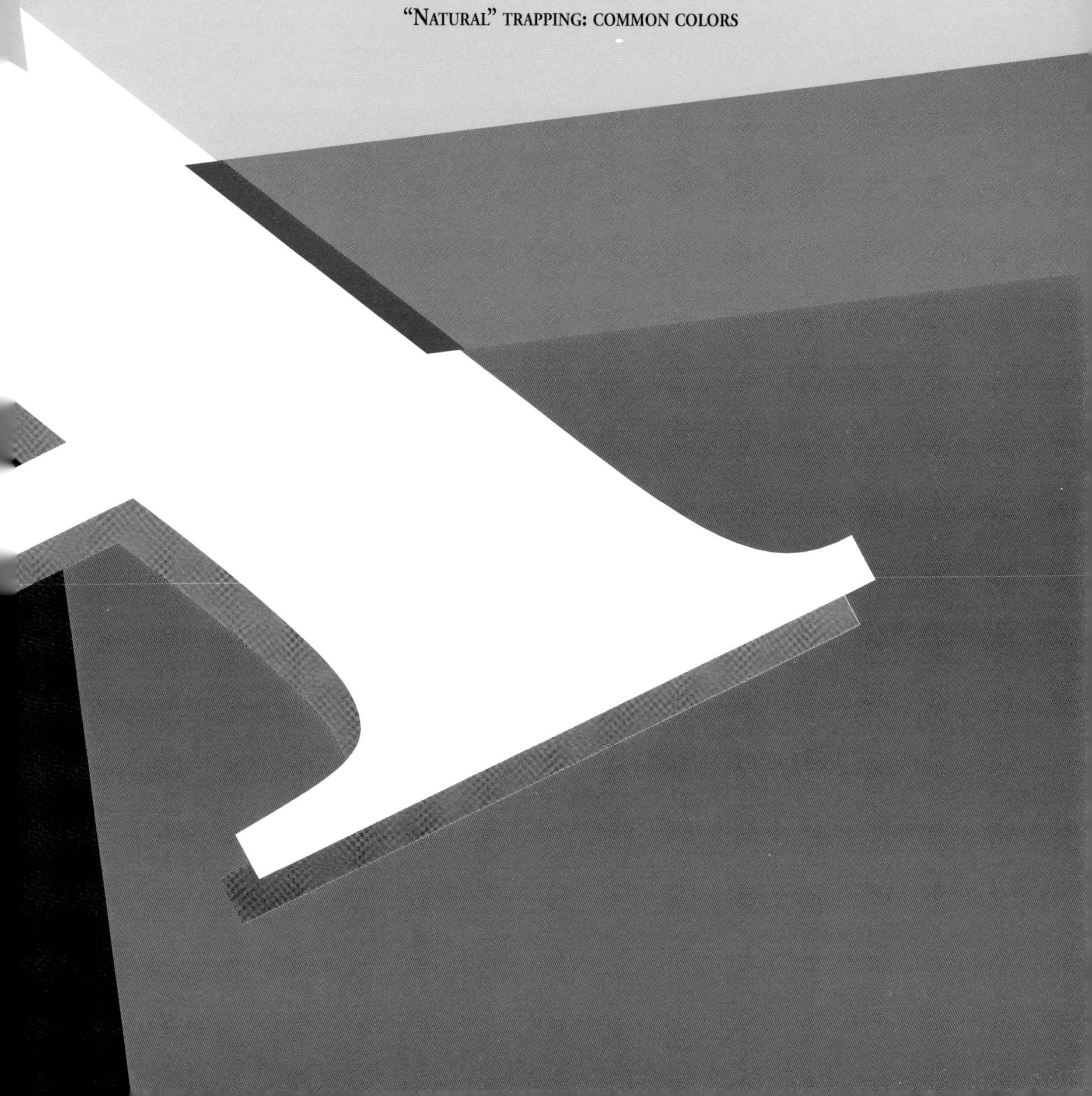

The ever-increasing versatility and sophistication of graphic design and desktop publishing programs have not only revolutionized the graphic arts industry, they've also revolutionized the way designers think of themselves. Today's designers and publishers are always hungry for additional graphic capabilities, because there's ultimately little distinction between what they and the software they own can do.

It's no surprise, then, that designers are frustrated by the limitations a printer can impose in order to meet a budget. Designers tend to want more tints, halftones, and color photos than they can afford, while printers are merely struggling to keep up with skyrocketing costs. To wit, everybody wants more control than they've got, and the thorny issues of trapping only serve to aggravate this problem.

There are, quite simply, two ways to avoid trapping: first by delegation, or second by design. In this chapter, we'll examine what happens when trapping work is passed on to a printer or prepress firm (delegation) and how artwork can be created without the need for trapping at all (design).

TRAPPING AT THE PRINTER OR PREPRESS SERVICE

When a designer or publisher delivers line art to a printer, the printer photographs it and creates a set of film negatives and overlays to make the printing plates. The printer controls the entire process, and is able to make film traps by photomechanical means. However, when film is delivered complete with screen tints, photos, and color separations, there's almost nothing the printer can do to improve the film with trapping techniques. The printer's hands are tied, and the designer or publisher becomes the bad guy when the final product isn't acceptable.

Desktop prepress may give designers the control to add as many tints, halftones, and color images as they want, and as many complex color interactions as they can create, but it works perfectly only if the designer takes full responsibility for providing workable film. That means the film both fits and traps perfectly. If this is beyond your studio's resources or personnel, you're better off allowing the printer to have total control—even if it hurts to give it up.

With the arrival of software trapping solutions, more and more printing companies and prepress firms with PostScript imagesetters now offer trapping as an extra-cost option at the time of film production. These firms have invested in trapping software and hardware to make the process of film production more successful.

By choosing a printing or prepress firm that has knowledge of trapping and has trapping capabilities in-house, a graphic artist can design to his or her heart's content, then send the complete color document to such a firm for trapping and completion. Then the process of trapping can be done by experienced technicians, leaving the design process in the hands of talented people who need only understand the *concept* of trapping and where it is required in their projects.

Again, a word of caution: If you decide to delegate trapping responsibility to outside suppliers, you must be sure to communicate your needs and deadlines early and clearly. Trapping affects price, production time, and delivery schedules, so your printer or prepress service must have adequate advance notice.

DOING IT YOURSELF

Some designers create pages without adjoining or overlapping elements, eliminating, the need for trapping altogether. Many designers consider this technique too conservative and creatively limiting, but it is a perfectly legitimate way to banish all worries about trapping. Here are a few ways for you to create trap-free designs:

Overprinting: no knockout, no trapping

When multiple colors overprint, the potential for trapping is completely eliminated. However, a factor to consider with this technique is that overprinting creates new colors. For example, printing magenta over cyan will create purple in those areas where overprinting takes place. Such derived colors may not create an attractive combination in the project's overall appearance, and may make it impossible to use the overprint technique.

On the other hand, if the color created by overprinting is anticipated in the design of the project, and that color does not cause unattractive intersections of colors, then the solution to trapping for the project is at hand.

Most desktop design and page layout programs default to "knockout" colors from one another. The result is an unprinted hole in the surrounding color that is exactly the size of the second color. This is the very condition that creates the potential for misregistration on the printing press and creates the situation addressed by trapping.

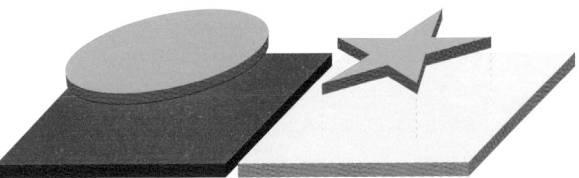

An alternative to the knockout approach to printing is to design projects that overprint. Overprinting creates new colors, but requires no trapping. In the examples shown, the cyan artwork overprints the magenta and yellow colors. Overprinting is typically possible as an option in page layout and desktop design programs.

The resulting colors change to a deep blue (some would call it purple), left, and bright green, right. There is no opportunity for press register error, and therefore no trapping is needed. Overprinting as a policy is an excellent technique for printing, but requires careful planning to allow for the combined colors created when two—or more—images are overprinted.

An example of an illustration trapped entirely by a web of black overprint lines. This technique, common to comic book and similar art, relies on black to trap all the color, and it works well as long as all the colors can be outlined with black.

There's one catch to this "simple" solution: Many PostScript separation programs will automatically overprint black. By overprinting black, type (which usually prints in black) and all other black information requires no trapping. If you want black not to overprint, you must take steps to avoid it.

Colors intended to overprint must be instructed to do so with the software controls in a given program, because PostScript does not overprint as a matter of course; in fact PostScript does the opposite. Any object that superimposes another object by default will be opaque, creating an opening in the object below to accommodate it. If you give this some thought, this makes perfect sense, otherwise all objects would be transparent, resulting in a mishmash of information on the page.

Designers occasionally use a clever method of creating *non-overprinting* black. In illustration programs they create a custom process color. This color can be named "black2" or "ebony" and designated as 100 percent black.

PostScript color separation programs use a technique called *parsing* to look through the file and overprint all items which are colored "black." If you use "ebony," the color isn't "black" so no overprint will take place where that color is used. The "ebony" elements will print on the black plate along with black elements created in XPress or elsewhere. With QuarkXPress's ability to specify whether each element will overprint or not (version 3.1 and later in the Trap Information window), the creation of such custom colors is optional.

Some programs like PrePrint Pro from Adobe Systems give you the option of declaring black to either overprint or not. Note in this case, however, that *all* the black components will either overprint or not overprint. Adobe Separator (versions 3.01 and later) will not overprint black unless the color has been declared to overprint in Adobe Illustrator's Paint dialog box on an object-by-object basis. Separator thus treats black as opaque, the same as any other color unless the operator holds down the Option key (on the Macintosh version) when printing from Separator, in which case black can be instructed to overprint.

Some designs lend themselves to black overprint trapping. If a design has a black outline around all color elements, that black line can be used to trap colors. Comic book art and illustrated novels provide a good example of how black can be used to trap all the color of an illustration. This is a reasonable technique for avoiding trapping difficulties.

"Natural" trapping: common colors

Combining colors is a simple and elegant way to work around the trapping problem. If you learn to think as a color strategist, and you build colors that contain common denominators, you can forget about trapping for this particular project.

These two intersecting colors present a potential for press register error. By adding a small percentage of one color to the other, that potential can be reduced or eliminated. Here, 20 percent of yellow is added to the cyan in the right hand image, reducing the problem of register error. Care must be taken to choose the color to make common, as unattractive results are likely; in this case, adding cyan to the yellow would have produced a pale green—a less attractive color than the yellow-supplemented cyan.

For example, a client has asked for a nautical flag to be printed on a page. The flag has light blue and yellow colors. Using pure cyan with pure yellow can result in a trapping problem at the intersection. But, adding just 20 percent yellow to the cyan eliminates the need for a trap because the tint of yellow is common to both the cyan and the yellow.

It takes about 20 percent of any color to make an effective trap-preventing common color, otherwise the tint that shows in the event of a press error is so light that it's as bad as plain paper showing through.

If black is one of the colors in the multi-color intersection, it can be used as a solid or as a screen tint to create a common-color trap. To introduce black, or any other color which does not have one of the intersecting colors as its base color to make a trap is counterproductive. This will only create more potential for register error.

One of the beneficial side effects of using common colors is the creation of a palette of coordinated colors that work together both aesthetically and for trapping purposes.

These colors must be trapped			These colors need no trapping		Color added to accomplish "natural" color trap
First color	Second color	Resulting trap color	First color	Second color	
100C	100M	100M 100C	100C 20M	100M	20M
100M	100Y	100M 100Y	100M 10Y	100Y 10M	10M 10Y
100Y	100C	100C 100Y	100C 20Y	100Y	20Y
100K	100C	100C 100K	100K 20C	100C	20C
100C 100Y	100M	100C 100M 100Y	100C 100Y	100M 20Y	20Y

"Natural" trapping colors allow a graphic designer to produce a job without concern for trapping or register error. It takes only a small percentage of common color to prevent—or at least reduce—register error from showing up as an unsightly line of unprinted paper.

The chances of getting good results with no trapping are pretty slim; it is far better to take advantage of the technology available to make printing projects more successful through correct trapping.

5 Special Trapping Situations

TRAPPING BACKGROUNDS AND TEXT

SMALL TYPE

DISPLAY TYPE

OVERPRINTING TYPE

TRAPPING PHOTOS

TRAPPING PHOTOS INTO OTHER PHOTOS

TRAPPING GRADATIONS

GRADATIONS INTO SOLIDS

GRADATIONS INTO GRADATIONS

TRAPPING FOR FLEXOGRAPHIC PRINTING

The real challenge of trapping is in the exceptions, not in the everyday problems. This chapter will look at the many unique, case-by-case situations that occur in printing, and how trapping can best be adjusted to allow for them.

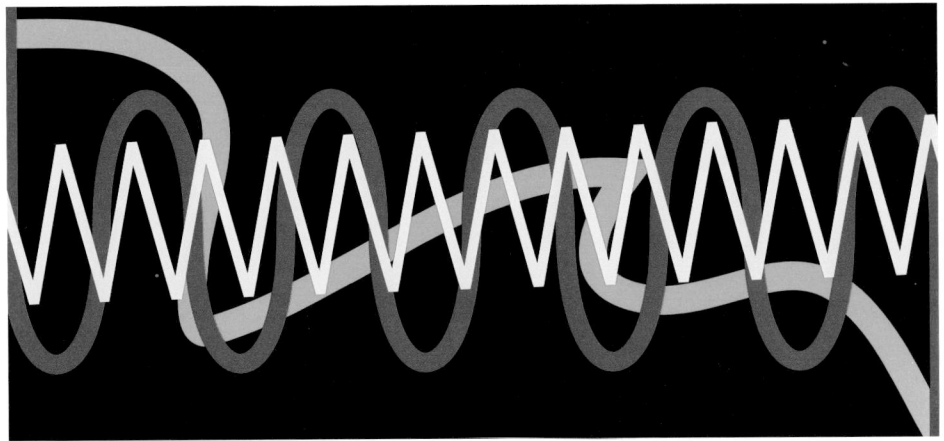

This particular example of art that requires trapping is most challenging, since all the colors intersect each other, and in every combination. While it would be possible to trap using manual techniques, complex trapping situations such as this are made easier by using electronic trapping products.

TRAPPING BACKGROUNDS AND TEXT

Small type

When building traps for small type, legibility and attractiveness are the goals to keep in mind. Whatever its color, small type should be left alone in a trapping situation with the opposing color choked into the type. However, there may be a situation where small type in a light color abuts a background of a much darker color. In this case it is perfectly safe to spread the type into the background, because the definition of the type will be made by the dark background, not by the light lettering color.

What is most important when dealing with information that carries the detail of an image (usually type, but often illustrative material), is that the detailed image be respected for its informational value. Spreading type into a background can often result in the type becoming unattractive or illegible. When that happens, the communicative value of the printed piece is lost and the reader moves on.

Note

Trapping software will often allow the user to establish a lower trap limit using a rule-based algorithm that dictates how much area to trap relative to a stroke thickness. This calculation eliminates the problem of trapped type becoming illegible as a result of trapping. A more detailed discussion of trapping software capabilities is available in Chapter 7, "Working with Dedicated Trapping Software."

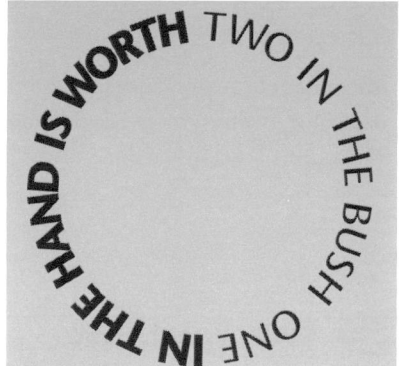 

Trapping type into various background colors can pose some interesting problems. On the left, cyan is usually considered the darker of the two colors, so it would spread under the magenta. But it might be better to do the opposite in order to keep the lettering from being damaged by the trap. The illustration is split, the left half showing that spread, the right side showing the opposite. On the right, the "darker" of the two colors is arguable. One could spread either one into the other, but the objective should be to hold the integrity of the lettering. Again, half of the illustration is trapped by spreading the pale blue, the other half is trapped by spreading the pale yellow (both colors are screen tints of the solid process colors).

Type printed on a **color background** should be treated **with care.** If you choke the **type with the** wrong color, or if **you choke too much,** the thin strokes **of the letters** will disappear!

For this example, too much trapping was set, and the thin strokes of the lettering disappeared in the process of trapping. To avoid this problem, the yellow should be spread under the blue, not the opposite, to let the darker color define the letter shapes while letting the lighter color do the trapping.

Display type

All the rules of normal trapping apply to display type, distinguished as measuring 24 points or more—with the notable exception of type with thin strokes or serifs that would disappear if trapped into neighboring colors. Large type is easy to trap by spreading the lighter color into the darker, resulting in a surrounding hairline of color. While this result cannot be avoided in every case, a reduction in the value of the trap color to 20 or 30 percent of its full value will correspondingly reduce the outlining effect dramatically.

Another approach is to choose common colors. Changing either the background color or the color of the type (with the client's approval, of course) to a color that traps naturally—this is always a simple solution.

OVERPRINTING TYPE

Quite often type can be declared to overprint, which eliminates the need to trap the type. Since most type is printed in the dominant color (usually black), the overprint technique is a simple solution to most trapping problems.

The lettering on the left knocks-out of the magenta background while the letters on the right overprint. The knock-out letters create an opportunity for register error while the overprint creates no such opportunity. But—the letters on the left maintain their cyan color, while the overprint letters become very dark blue as a result of the cyan-magenta overprint.

Overprinting, however, has its own set of problems. Overprinting colors other than black creates new colors that are unattractive in the design. Making the decision to overprint should always involve a consideration of the resulting color within the presentation of the overall printed work being created.

TRAPPING PHOTOS

Photo images should always be choked by the surrounding background color. The reason for this is simple: tonal matter in a photo changes from area to area, and the value or color of an image is an unreliable color with which to trap. Instead, choke the background color into the edge of the photo, or place a border around the photograph in design.

The most common border color for trapping photographs is an overprinting black. Black will bury almost all trapping problems with photographs and is a strong neutral color that usually takes nothing away from the photo.

When trapping color photographs, it is smart to use a rich black comprised of 100 percent black with 30 percent tints of cyan, yellow, and magenta added. This will trap all colors to each other, and will enrich the black at the same time.

Photo placed on top ——▶

Trapping line in background color ——▶

Window left for photo ◀——

Trapping photographs into backgrounds of color, or screen tints of black, is relatively easy. Leave a window in the background for the photo, then put a trapping line in the background color around the perimeter of the photograph that traps the photo.

Trapping photos into other photos

Photographs are usually random enough in color distribution that they do not need to be trapped. For trapping average photos into other photos electronically, simply place one scanned image on top of another within the page layout program. The software in the imagesetter will merge the halftone patterns without difficulty.

If the photos being overlaid have *significantly* different colors at their intersecting edges (little or no common color), the designer can build a composite image in Photoshop containing both images; this will reduce the risk of register error. In a conventional stripping environment, this process is much more difficult, requiring that a set of trapping windows be made that intersect the two images by one-half a dot—a very tricky process.

Another benefit of the composite photo technique is that the composite image turns out to be considerably smaller in file size than the total of the images used to create it. This makes the master file more portable and easier to work with both in the studio and at the printer or prepress firm.

Note

Remember that the options for moving, scaling, and cropping in a composite image are eliminated during the process of creating the master photo. It is wise to save all the original contributing photos so that repairs or revisions can be made if necessary.

An Illinois graphic designer who does a great deal of retail color advertising using the computer creates composite images because they cause less trouble. Says she, "I only have to worry about getting one placed file to the service bureau, and that way I never forget an all-important photo.

"There's nothing worse than getting a call from the service bureau telling you that the image of the motorcycle is missing. You miss your deadline, you have to buy color separations that you can't use, and you make everyone mad at you all at the same time!

"On one recent job—an 11" × 14"—I had a single full-bleed composite photo for the entire page. It was 23 megabytes in size, compared to almost 75 megabytes if I had included all the images that made up the composite."

TRAPPING GRADATIONS

Gradations into solids

Gradations cause unique trapping problems. It is impractical to trap a gradation with another gradation, so it's best to trap the background into the gradation (choke) regardless of its luminosity.

In a situation where a light value gradation is printed inside a darker color background, the darker background should be choked into the gradation. Even though this violates the principles of choosing the lighter color to do the work, it's just easier to accomplish a good trap using this method.

Gradations into gradations

Designers who use gradations on top of other gradations face the biggest potential problems. Trapping with an outline of a single color common to both colors is easy, though it may not be possible to find. Examining the available common colors to try to introduce a new color into both gradations that will be present at all values in the image is a viable alternative.

To trap a gradation into a solid, create a trapping outline in the background color. That way the gradation of colors will always trap with the background color. In this example, a cyan trap line is used because solid cyan is present at all values of the gradation.

For example, a background color of 20 percent cyan could be introduced under a gradation from yellow to magenta. This particular example would cause the yellow to go toward green, and the red toward violet, but the 20 percent cyan would be present at all values under the gradation, and is a suitable solution to the trapping of the image in question (although it creates a color combination that may be unacceptable).

In some cases the introduction of a tint of black under both gradations will create the common-color trap needed to prevent register
error. The black will darken all the values in the gradations, but it is a
neutral "color" that will not shift the hue of either gradation.

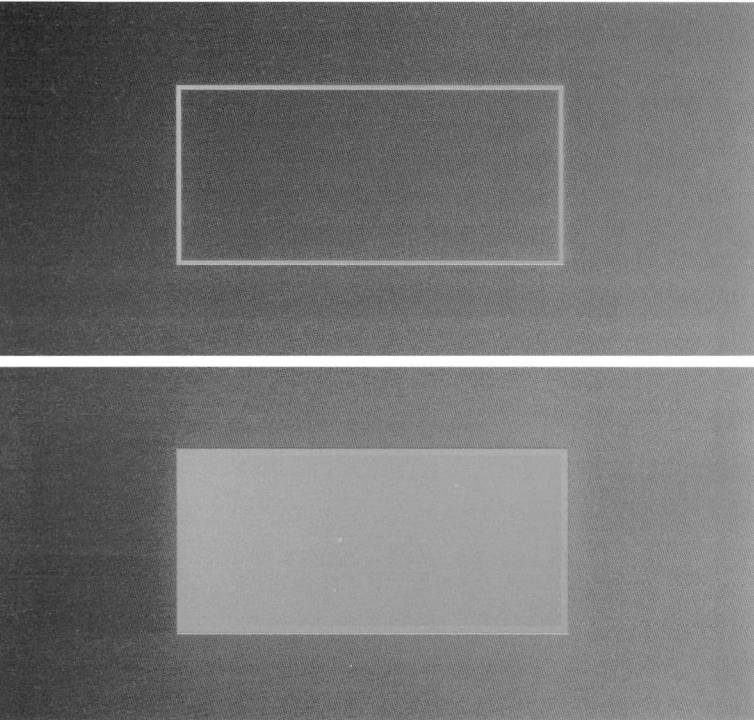

*Trapping a gradation into another gradation can be incredibly difficult, especially if
there are no colors common to the two gradations. To trap these two gradations successfully (in this case by using Illustrator 5.5), the outline path of the gradation was
converted into an object filled with the same gradation. That object is designated to
overprint, creating the necessary trap at all points of the two gradations. Using desktop
publishing and graphic design software to trap images is covered more thoroughly in
Chapter 6, "Trapping on the Desktop."*

Another approach to gradation trapping is to kiss-fit the gradation
into the other gradation (don't trap) and let the imagesetter do its
work. If the two gradations are made of the same colors, the trapping
error potential is small, occurring only at the point in the passing
gradations where there is no common color, or the common color is
so light in value that it would make an ineffective trap.

A final suggestion for gradation-to-gradation trapping is to create gradations that do not descend to zero value for either or both colors. This technique can leave a common color present at all values of the gradation, virtually eliminating the potential for register error because white (unprinted paper) is absent from the equation. In practice this means declaring the end value for the gradation to 10 or 20 percent of a color instead of zero.

TRAPPING FOR FLEXOGRAPHIC PRINTING

Flexographic printing has special trapping requirements, especially when it is used for packaging. Flexography generally requires larger traps than offset printing—typically 0.006 to 0.01 of an inch in flexo work as opposed to 0.003 to 0.006 of an inch in offset.

This difference is due to the added imprecision caused by printing on a variety of materials other than normal printing paper and to the generally larger number of colors used and the higher speed of the flexo press. Some flexo presses use opaque inks, rather than the transparent inks used on most offset presses. In addition, flexo printing usually involves multiple spot colors—sometimes eight or more. The order in which these colors is laid down is up to the printing firm and can affect trapping decisions. Here, again, communication with the printer is critical to determine the correct method for artwork preparation.

Flexography is very often used to print on non-white materials. As a result, opaque white ink may be the first color printed prior to printing the other colors. Another factor contributing to the preparation of art for flexographic printing is that each ink is dried between press units, allowing for heavier and more opaque coverage.

Flexo printing on packaging sometimes involves intentional curvilinear distortion for printing on formed plastic cups or bottles, where intersecting colors along a curve can be more challenging to keep in register.

6
Trapping on the Desktop

POSTSCRIPT DRAWING PROGRAMS

ADOBE ILLUSTRATOR

MACROMEDIA FREEHAND

CORELDRAW! AND OTHER ILLUSTRATION PROGRAMS

TRAPPING NEGATIVE SPACES

QUARKXPRESS AND ADOBE PAGEMAKER

PHANTOM TRAPS: SPREADS AND ILLUSTRATIONS

ADOBE PHOTOSHOP

TRAPPING ON COLOR ELECTRONIC PREPRESS SYSTEMS

As page layout and graphic design programs have evolved into more sophisticated products, each subsequent upgrade adds new and more powerful features to the designer's toolbox. Many of these programs now include trapping capabilities or work-arounds that can be used to create trapped art for printing.

QuarkXPress 3.0 features a varied set of trapping functions, capable of trapping text and graphic elements, although only those created within the program. Adobe Illustrator and Macromedia FreeHand can be used to create fully trapped illustrations. CorelDRAW! can also be used to trap artwork manually. Adobe Illustrator ships with a trapping filter and Adobe PageMaker 6.0 features an addition called TrapMaker that does trapping at the time of printing to a PostScript printer or imagesetter.

The reality, however, is that even automatic trapping in page layout and graphic design programs can't handle the bulk of trapping requirements. None of these programs can automatically trap all the varied elements within a page design, whether they be illustrations, drawings, graduated fills, scan files, or other artwork. Within each of these elements, traps must be created in their native environments, followed by additional traps to be applied according to the final arrangement of the page. The would-be desktop trapper has to look into each of the available programs and examine their individual trapping capabilities.

POSTSCRIPT DRAWING PROGRAMS

There's one hard and fast rule in desktop trapping: Always remember that when you take up the responsibility for trapping in a PostScript environment, *it's all yours* —no matter what comes out the other end. With the help of such programs you can trap both text and other vector-based objects and the results can be completely successful. But never forget trapping is a serious responsibility, and it must be done with great care and attention to detail in order to work out well in the end.

The PostScript paths drawn by Adobe Illustrator and Macromedia FreeHand— and other similar illustration programs—follow the characteristics of the path shown here, with the theoretical path passing down the exact center of the full stroke. Half of the value of the stroke is drawn on either side of the path line.

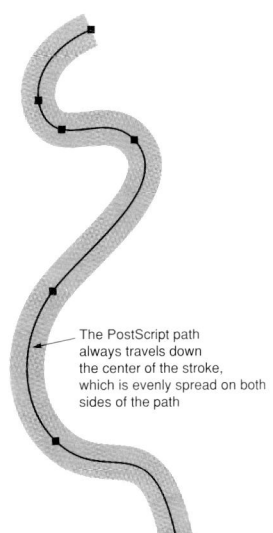

The PostScript path always travels down the center of the stroke, which is evenly spread on both sides of the path

Adobe Illustrator

Adobe Illustrator boasts several important trapping capabilities via Pathfinder technology, including the ability to crop, converge, and clip paths; the analysis of edge intersections; and the acceptance plug-ins like trapping. Trapping works only on *closed* paths in Illustrator; text must first be converted to outlines, and open strokes must be converted to closed paths—another Pathfinder feature.

Adobe Illustrator's Trap filter is accessed from the Filter>Pathfinder menu in the menu bar. Pathfinder technology makes trapping possible through its ability to create paths parallel to existing paths, and to convert open paths into solid objects.

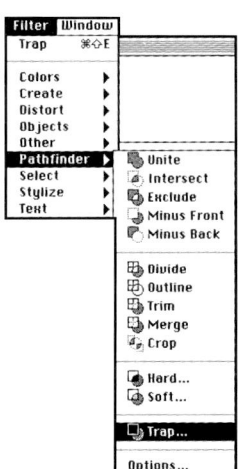

Trapping with Illustrator results in files that can be saved in EPS format and placed into PageMaker or QuarkXPress, and which will trap on output from those page layout programs. (Don't scale these illustrations in page layout! Scaling will change the size of trapping lines, and can ruin the printed piece.) However, the combination of Illustrator-trapped elements and either PageMaker or QuarkXPress with their trapping functions, can be a solution to the overall problem of trapping for many designers.

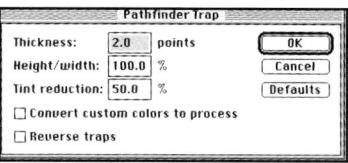

Adobe Illustrator's Trap filter provides settings for trap size, a height/width ratio control, and tint reduction percentage. The height/width ratio will create traps that have different values horizontally and vertically. Tint reduction lessons the intensity of traps created between elements, making their color less prominent. The Reverse traps button will reverse the direction traps go, dominant into subordinate.

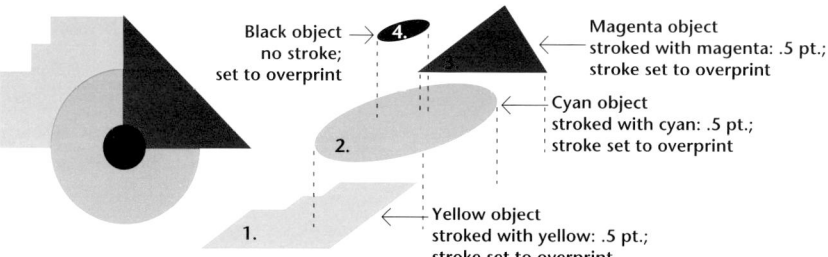

Trapping in illustration programs typically involves assigning a stroke to any object that should be trapped. These trapping lines should be assigned a color—typically the subordinate color—and declared to overprint in the program's object attributes window. This example shows all objects stroked except the black circle, which is set to overprint.

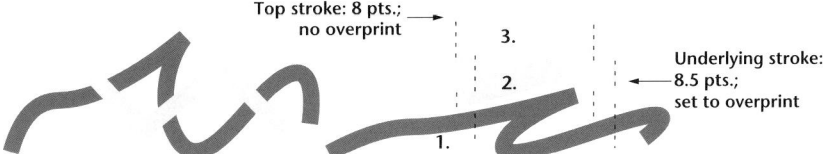

Top stroke: 8 pts.;
no overprint

3.

2.

1.

Underlying stroke:
8.5 pts.;
set to overprint

Paths must be duplicated in illustration programs to create trapping lines. Each path that must trap should have an exact duplicate (some programs call this a clone) *underlying it. That path should be stroked thicker than the top path, and set to overprint. This will create a trapping line for a path over another path or any object.*

Macromedia FreeHand

FreeHand now has an automatic trapping function, the latest addition in the battle for features. In addition to this internal function, anyone with Adobe Illustrator and FreeHand can use Illustrator's Trapping plug-in in FreeHand, which now accepts Illustrator's entire array of plug-in filters.

Macromedia FreeHand 5 offers trapping as a semi-automatic function. The trap control window, shown here, is capable of making some impressive traps. Interestingly, FreeHand also supports the plug-in filters from Adobe Illustrator, making Illustrator's trapping filter accessible to FreeHand.

CorelDRAW! and other illustration programs

When using CorelDRAW! to spread an object—as an example—you can choose that object and apply a stroke to it in the same color as the basic object. The stroke must be declared to overprint, and must be set to a line thickness that is double the thickness of the intended trap.

Why double the thickness? PostScript paths are theoretical curves. When stroked with any color, half of the color extends on one side of the path while the other half extends out from the other side of the path. To set a trap thickness of 0.003 of an inch, you would have to enter a thickness of 0.006 of an inch. If your illustration application accepts line thicknesses in points only, you must calculate what 0.006 of an inch equals in points. To get the answer you want, you divide the trap (already doubled) by 0.0138; the product is the stroke thickness in points.

A designer knowledgeable in the concepts of trapping can apply overprinting strokes to any object that will perform the task of trapping on press. Object stroking is simple, though open paths (lines that are not closed into objects) require more work; any open path to be trapped must be duplicated, and the duplicate path must be declared to overprint at the proper line weight to accomplish the task.

Trapping with illustration programs is relatively easy, but time consuming. In addition, proofing the traps is extraordinarily important; errors can occur while creating traps in any environment, and illustration programs offer ample opportunity for such problems.

One Pennsylvania service bureau owner notes that about half the jobs he gets now that have been trapped by owners have problems. "The problem," he says, "is not usually in trapping the wrong objects, it's not understanding how the underlying principles work. Many designers don't understand the PostScript stroke command."

Trapping negative spaces

Artwork that reverses out of solid areas—typically black or rich black—poses another problem for trapping. When dealing with artwork that reverses out of heavy solids, the trapping problem is likewise reversed, and your trapping strategy must take into account the potential "leakage" of one color under the others due to misregistration on press. The trapping technique used in this situation is called a *keepaway*. Another term for the same procedure is *hold back*. The objective is to hold back the colors—other than the black—so that the detail is defined only by the process black, and to prevent individual colors from peeking out from under the black in circumstances of misregistration.

Trapping for negative spaces requires a different approach. Colors common to the background color must be held back from the detailed part of the image. In this example, all the process colors are kept away from the reverse lettering. Only the black ink defines the actual letterforms.

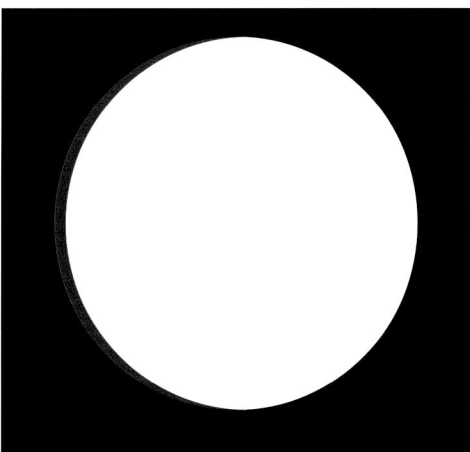

Register errors in reverse images show up as colors peeking out from behind the image.

In conventional film preparation, the keepaway is produced by spreading a positive film of the reversed item, then using that spread to mask the colors while the original positive masks only the black. As mentioned, the weight of this keepaway is significantly heavier than a similar spread trap would be in positive areas. Because it reverses out of black, the effect usually does not show.

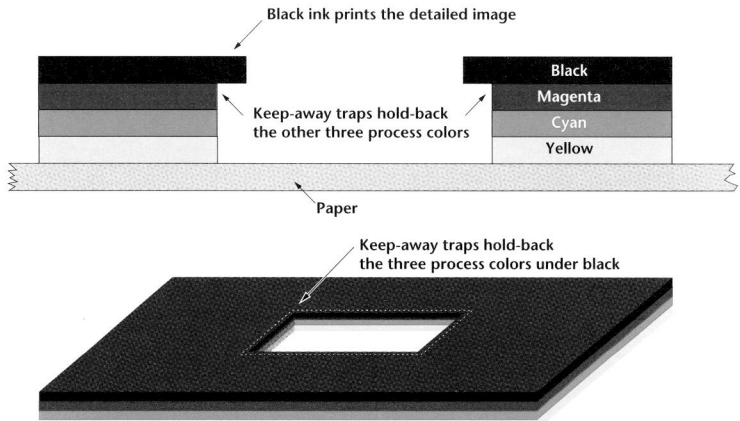

Here is a greatly enlarged side view of the technique of keeping colors away from the black detail.

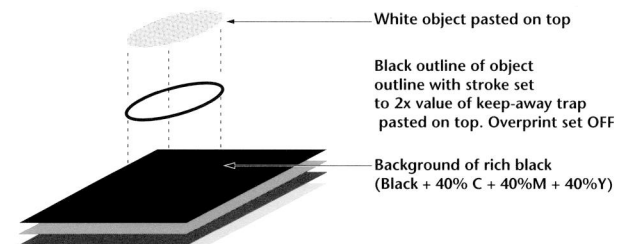

The keepaway technique in perspective: follow this method when creating keepaways in illustration programs. Notice that overprint is set off for the trapping line—the opposite of trapping a positive object. This causes the colors to be set back from the edge of the image. Black becomes the defining color at the edge of the image—in this case, an elliptical object.

When preparing keepaways for printing, it is best to consult with your printer to determine his or her desired keepaway trap value. A sketch is often helpful in ensuring that correct communication is accomplished—especially because the technique carries so many different names and units of measure.

The preparation of manual keepaways in electronic prepress requires good planning because of the sometimes-confusing combination of elements involved. In illustration programs, when preparing trapping for reverse elements, the keepaways must be handled much differently than for positive areas.

First, an area of solid or rich black must be created, followed by the element to be reversed. This element is stroked with black at double the usual trap value (check with the printer for the correct value) and the overprint option is not selected. Then a copy of the same element must be pasted on top and set to be filled white with no stroke.

Reversing-out to colors other than black requires that the fill of the reversed element be set to the chosen color; the stroke must be the same color with no overprint. The copy that is pasted on top is then filled with the chosen color only, with no stroke.

Keepaways are particularly useful when type with thin strokes is reversed out of rich colors, and where the misregistration of any single color would damage or obliterate the thin strokes of the letters in the reverse.

TRAPPING SCORECARD **ILLUSTRATION PRODUCTS**	MANUAL TRAPPING	AUTOMATIC TRAPPING	PRECISE TRAPPING POSSIBLE	EASY TO DO TRAPPING	SOPHISTICATED TRAPPING
ADOBE ILLUSTRATOR	✔	✔	✔	✔	✔
MACROMEDIA FREEHAND	✔	✔	✔	✔	✔
CORELDRAW!	✔		✔		✔
MICROGRAFX DESIGNER	✔		✔		✔

QUARKXPRESS AND ADOBE PAGEMAKER

QuarkXPress versions 3.0 and higher have built-in automatic and semi-automatic trapping. QuarkXPress can trap any object, image, or text *that is created within the program.* Illustrations from Illustrator and FreeHand are not trapped by QuarkXPress, nor are any other images imported into the program, though these illustrations can be trapped upstream, and imported already-trapped into QuarkXPress.

QuarkXPress' default trap setting is 0.144 point. This can be permanently changed by the user to any value in QuarkXPress' Preferences menu. The functionality of QuarkXPress trapping is good, and the user can edit the color trapping values and methods for most combinations of color intersections.

QuarkXPress has a Trap Information window that can be opened on the document layout at any time. This window shows the value and type of trap for any selected object. Settings can be overridden by the user to choke (a negative value) or spread (a positive value) in any increment. In addition, an object can be declared to overprint.

There are some trap situations that cannot be overridden by the user, or where the program reverts its trap selection to "indeterminate" after the user selects the override. Future versions of QuarkXPress will likely address those few situations where user override is not currently possible.

QuarkXPress can create functional traps for most situations including reverse images where keepaway traps are required. QuarkXPress knows that it must keep process colors back from the detail image that is printed by the black ink, and it creates traps appropriate to this purpose. Tests of rich blacks indicate that the program will create precise keepaways for reversed images.

Users are cautioned to be meticulous about the placement of all objects and windows in QuarkXPress; it is important not to leave any unused text or graphic objects on the page, and it is equally important to be sure that only the colors used in the job are left in the color palette when printing to color separated film. The four process colors will remain in all jobs, as do the colors named *Registration* and *White.* Others not used should be deleted, and spot colors intended for separation as process color separations must have the *Process Separation* button checked in the Edit Colors dialog box.

```
┌─────────────────────────────────────────────────┐
│ ▓▓▓▓▓▓▓▓▓▓▓▓  Aldus® TrapMaker™  ▓▓▓▓▓▓▓▓▓▓▓▓    │
│                                                   │
│  Default width:  [0.0035]  in      ┌───────────┐ │
│                                    │  Print...  │ │
│                                    └───────────┘ │
│  Black width:    [0.0069]  in      ┌───────────┐ │
│                                    │   Done    │ │
│                                    └───────────┘ │
│  Trap text over:     [12]  pts     ┌───────────┐ │
│                                    │  Cancel   │ │
│                                    └───────────┘ │
│  Black limit:       [100]  %                      │
│                                    ┌───────────┐ │
│  Centerline threshold: [70]  %     │ Overrides..│ │
│                                    └───────────┘ │
│  Step limit:         [10]  %       ┌───────────┐ │
│                                    │ Ink setup..│ │
│                                    └───────────┘ │
│                                    ┌───────────┐ │
│                                    │   Help... │ │
│                                    └───────────┘ │
│                                    ┌───────────┐ │
│                                    │  About... │ │
│                                    └───────────┘ │
└─────────────────────────────────────────────────┘
```

TrapMaker, an Addition for PageMaker and one of the Adobe Open prepress products, allows impressive control over the traps created. The TrapMaker Addition will only trap items created in PageMaker, and only when printing takes place from PageMaker.

PageMaker features the ability to add software plug-ins, called Additions, to the program. An Addition for trapping called TrapMaker adds trapping functions to PageMaker that are similar to those of QuarkXPress. The TrapMaker Addition ships with PageMaker 6.0.

TrapMaker functions are implemented by the PostScript printer. They are not added to the elements in the document. And, like QuarkXPress, elements imported into PageMaker from Illustrator or other applications are not trapped at all, because TrapMaker cannot distinguish the individual components of the illustration.

Previously trapped illustrations can be placed into PageMaker, and they will be dutifully trapped at the time of imagesetting; TrapMaker has no effect on these trapped illustrations.

Phantom traps: Spreads and illustrations

It is possible to create a spread in Illustrator or FreeHand that will trap to a QuarkXPress or PageMaker object once it is placed in that document. To accomplish this, create a stroked line of the correct trapping color around the perimeter of the illustration (you must know both colors in advance and choose the correct trapping color) and declare this trapping line to overprint in the illustration program. The line must have the correct thickness for a trap—even though the object into which it is trapping isn't present. (Illustrator's automatic trap plug-in will not create this trap automatically; you must do it manually, or trick the plug-in by first placing your illustration on a colored background, trapping, then removing the background.)

Once the illustration is complete, save it in EPS format, and place it into a QuarkXPress or PageMaker page on top of the background color intended. You can also place the illustration over a photograph in QuarkXPress. The image will appear to be too fat at the border; this is a result of the software's inability to display traps correctly. But when the image is color-separated to film, the trapping line will over-print correctly and will result in trapping that is correct.

Note

As already mentioned, imported graphics will not be trapped by QuarkXPress or PageMaker. In order for illustrative material to trap internally, it must be trapped in the original program *at its final size* (or the whole job must be trapped electronically later). This trapping must be done by hand. Scaling in page layout programs will proportionately change the thickness of the traps in the illustration with potentially damaging results.

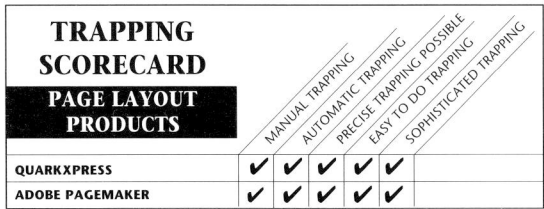

ADOBE PHOTOSHOP

Photoshop is almost universally used to edit color and monochrome images, can trap any image within its wide range of document types. When working with a CMYK image, Photoshop offers a Trap dialog box. When selected, the user is prompted for the amount of trap, measured in pixels, points, or millimeters. This value is mathematically converted and rounded to a whole number trap value in pixels, and the program makes the trapping intersections. It does so by additive mathematics, making the trap color between two colors equal to the total of their colors.

Trapping in Photoshop is rarely done, and usually results in odd color trap lines. Unless you specifically need to trap an Illustrator document using Photoshop, the resulting quality problems and huge file sizes do not justify the effort. Using Photoshop should be considered an alternate solution to using the other desktop software programs listed here—for the occasional inter-photo trapping when two drastically different (hue differences) images intersect.

Test Squares trapped using Adobe Photoshop 3.0. Photoshop rasterizes the PostScript file to final resolution, then builds traps as a bitmap modification in the file. The file must remain a bitmap to print, as there is no way to convert to EPS illustration format from Photoshop.

Note

A little-known feature of Photoshop is its ability to read and rasterize files from Adobe Illustrator. Rasterization converts these files from Illustrator's native file format to a bitmap (a picture). This picture can then be trapped using Photoshop's trapping function, and printed as a color separation from Photoshop (or QuarkXPress, or PrePrint, or other color separation programs).

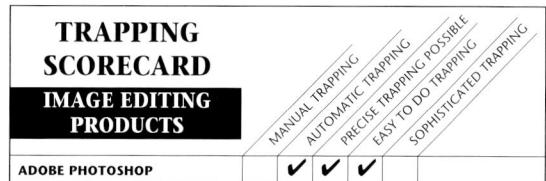

TRAPPING ON COLOR ELECTRONIC PREPRESS SYSTEMS

There is another alternative to trapping on desktop systems or on the light table: All of the major high-end prepress systems include links to desktop systems that make it possible to transfer files generated on a Macintosh computer for completion on the powerful color electronic prepress systems (CEPS) platforms. These systems are manufactured by Du Pont Imaging Systems (also called Crosfield in Canada, Asia, and Europe), Linotype-Hell, Scitex, and Screen (Dai Nippon Screen).

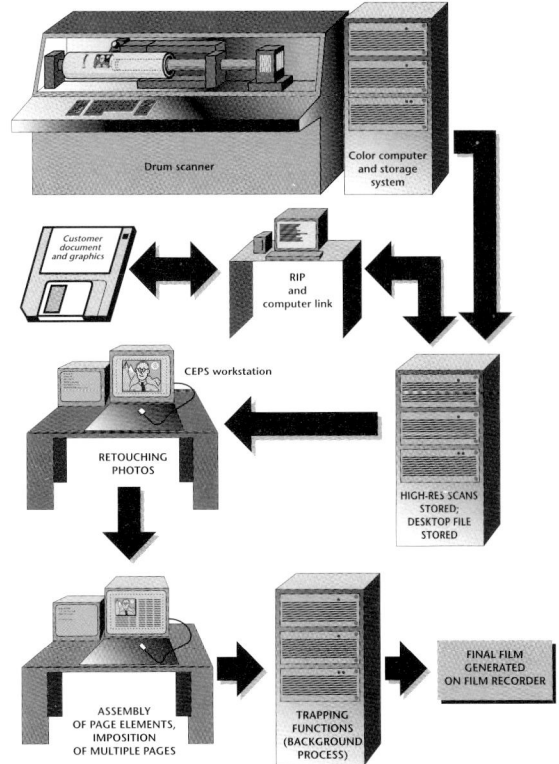

Color Electronic Prepress Systems (CEPS) can accept files from desktop systems using a technique called OPI (Open Prepress Interface). The system, shown here in flowchart form, can substitute high-resolution photographs for position-only images in the desktop files. Trapping is done at the bitmap level, after all page assembly and photo replacement is complete.

CEPS shops usually have an assortment of equipment, including at least one drum scanner, an array of high-speed disk systems, and one or more retouching and page assembly stations that handle the job of correcting and building complete pages of material for output as composite film. The link to the desktop publishing world is usually made by a dedicated computer connected to a Macintosh or PC. This dedicated computer performs the tasks of network transfer and PostScript rasterization. Rasterization is the process of converting the native language of desktop systems into the very high-resolution bitmapped files used by the color electronic prepress systems. These transfers accomplish the task of converting all of the artwork and type in a desktop project into the native language of the high-end color world.

The names for these systems vary from manufacturer to manufacturer: Du Pont's is named StudioLink; Linotype-Hell calls its system ScriptMaster; Scitex calls its system Visionary Gateway; Screen's is PS-I/Omega. All include a PostScript interpreter (software RIP) and the software necessary to convert the resulting raster files into the internal code of the high-end system. Once inside the CEPS, desktop files are treated like files scanned or generated on these systems.

One benefit of making a transfer to a CEPS is that the trapping capabilities of these systems are mature and highly effective. The ability to produce flawless trapped film for printing is a routine task for such systems. These systems typically trap at the bitmap level, creating new rows of color pixels that are comprised of color values needed to perform the trap.

High-end systems trap files at full resolution, lining the trapping edges of bitmapped areas with common color pixels to a width appropriate to the printing process selected. The operator must enter a trapping value, which is converted to whole number pixels by the system, and then used to establish the thickness of the trap areas.

A color look-up table is provided with the equipment. This table contains a grid of potential color intersections with recommended trapping colors and values. The operator, or a system administrator, has access to the look-up table, and can modify any color intersection for subsequent trapping. Extensive testing has gone into these look-up tables, and in most cases they provide reliable color traps.

The trapping functions are often completed as background tasks; by relegating the trapping of completed pages to background processing, operators are free to work on other projects that require their attention. In fact, CEPS trapping is a very powerful and effective method of producing trapped files.

The benefit of handling PostScript trapping on high-end systems is that it releases the designer from the need to understand or accept the liability for trapping. The quality of traps created by CEPS systems is unquestionably excellent. The process is relatively fast, and it results in a "no excuses" product that should print without any difficulty on press.

The other consideration is the hourly cost of production on such systems is quite high. At present, hourly rates range from $150–$300 per hour. These charges, in addition to the cost of generating film and proofs, can make the use of CEPS for trapping prohibitively expensive.

Interestingly, the technique that CEPS computers use to create traps in artwork is very similar to that used by the Photoshop program on the Macintosh, only with much more specialized trapping functions. While the high-end systems have accessible look-up tables for color selection (Photoshop does not), the technique involves drawing contours of trapping pixels on colors that overlap with other colors not sharing a common color.

The color value and depth of these intersections are controlled by the operator, who sets specifications for the printing process and halftone frequency. The halftone frequency value establishes the thickness of any trap created on such a system.

A caveat of trapping files on CEPS equipment is that reclaiming files once translated into the native language of the prepress system, is very costly and difficult to manage. Once in the prepress system, these files are huge bitmap files with geometry codes that are incompatible with desktop computers.

7

Working with Dedicated Trapping Software

ISLANDTRAPPER

ADOBE TRAPWISE

SCITEX DOLEV IMAGESETTERS

RAMPAGE RIPS

THE NECESSITY OF PROOFREADING

DALIM TRAPPING SYSTEM

Despite the fact that the authors of PostScript did not include trapping as a basic function of their page description language, the problem has been successfully addressed as a software function. A handful of commercial products now exist that solve the majority of trapping problems for the publishing industry.

Test Squares created in Adobe Illustrator 5.5. There is no trapping in this illustration, but many opportunities for register error on press.

ISLANDTRAPPER

Island Graphics Corporation has created IslandTrapper, the first Macintosh-based program for PostScript trapping. Using a technique for interpreting PostScript into an object display list, IslandTrapper uses vector analysis to trap any EPS file from any program, and prepare that file for output to an imagesetter.

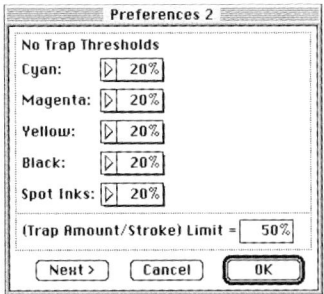

IslandTrapper Preferences allow the user to establish a variety of values. Three default thicknesses for trapping, no-trap thresholds (shown) and settings for hands-off trapping using its Hot Folder set-up. Hot Folders allow a user to drop any file needing trapping into a folder (or an alias of that folder) for trapping. The program will automatically trap the file, then place the trapped file into an "out basket" and the untouched original file into a folder called "originals."

```
OBJECTS: 66
TIME REQUIRED TO CHECK RESOURCES: 00:00:01
TIME REQUIRED TO LOAD: 00:00:04
TIME REQUIRED TO PREPARE CANVAS: 00:00:00
TOTAL TIME REQUIRED TO OPEN: 00:00:35
TIME REQUIRED TO VIEW SELECTED TRAPS: 00:00:00
TIME REQUIRED TO VIEW SELECTED TRAPS: 00:00:00
TIME REQUIRED TO VIEW SELECTED TRAPS: 00:00:01
TIME REQUIRED TO VIEW SELECTED TRAPS: 00:00:00
TIME REQUIRED TO VIEW SELECTED TRAPS: 00:00:31
TIME REQUIRED TO VIEW SELECTED TRAPS: 00:00:06
```

The Log file in IslandTrapper keeps track of all operations in the program. It keeps track of times for opening, trapping, viewing and saving, all of which can be helpful in billing for the service of trapping in the program. In this window, the Test Squares file was opened and trapped in a total of 0:40. Subsequent operations (preview and return to normal) took an additional 0:37.

Files to be trapped by IslandTrapper are saved as single-page EPS files, which are then processed by Trapper. The program has powerful features for global and local trapping, and object-by-object override when needed. It is capable of delivering first-rate trapped files to any PostScript imagesetter or to an imposition program that can create complete forms of pages ready for plate.

The Local Trap editor in IslandTrapper allows any individual combination of objects to be trapped with special considerations. This allows special circumstances to be accommodated without affecting other objects that may share the same colors.

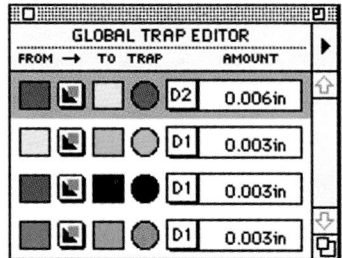

The Global Trap editor in IslandTrapper allows any pair of color intersections to be trapped differently than the logic of the program dictates. Once you have analyzed the trapping settings set by IslandTrapper, you can overrule, override, or remove traps for the entire document based on color intersections.

The most notable feature of IslandTrapper is its handling of objects, making them available to the operator (changes or corrections in color or trapping function are done in the Trapper program), and the sophisticated trap color and value selection process used by the program. Using a system of color edge analysis, the program creates vector trapping lines that, on output, are converted to PostScript code for the imagesetter.

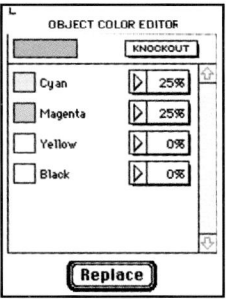

IslandTrapper's Object color editor allows any element in a page to be modified once it has been opened by Trapper. This allows for minor color corrections or changes in Trapper, obviating the need to return to the program that created the file to make the change.

IslandTrapper supports keepaway trapping for reverse areas, tint traps for subtle color intersections, spot color trapping with spot-to-process controls, sophisticated gradation trapping, with unlimited opportunity for operator intervention when required.

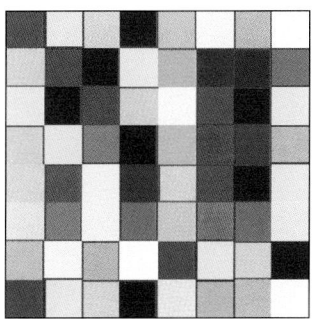

The Test Squares file opened in IslandTrapper, with preview turned on to "special." The setting for trap widths was changed to 0.02" to exaggerate the preview.

Version 2.0 is a Power PC-native, Macintosh-based program; it provides a solution to trapping that resides on the platform that is predominant in the PostScript output industry. Productivity in the processing of files is very good, and operator training and efficiency are simplified.

IslandTrapper includes a Quark XTension that makes the process of creating EPS files from QuarkXPress simpler. The XTension allows individual pages, or entire documents, to be made ready for Trapper from within QuarkXPress.

ADOBE TRAPWISE

Adobe Systems now offers a product called TrapWise, acquired during its merger with Aldus Corporation. The program is available for Macintosh and PC computers. Its features include an excellent user interface, and sophisticated error flagging.

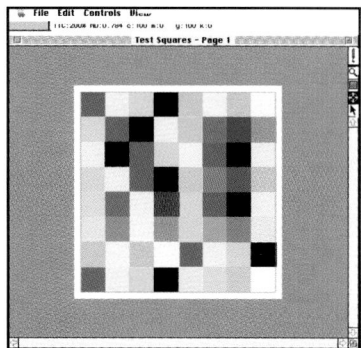

The TrapWise main window. TrapWise uses a software PostScript interpreter to raster-ize the file for color intersection analysis, then writes PostScript code to perform trap-ping on original file, discarding the rasterized information. Onscreen is a densitometer that provides color value and total ink coverage for any spot touched with the densito-meter tool.

TrapWise uses raster-based color edge analysis, then the program cre-ates supplemental PostScript code that is *appended* to the original PostScript file. The program's bit-map conversion of the file is made for color analysis only, and no changes are made to the original file whatsoever. Object positions and other attributes of the original EPS file are untouched.

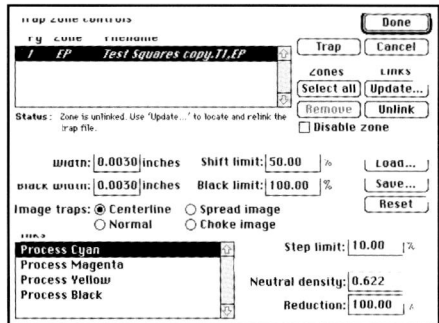

TrapWise offers controls for trap widths that affect the entire image, or for a zone with-in the image as defined by the Trap Zone tool. Items inside a rectangular zone are trapped with settings that can be independent of the balance of the page. In this image, the entire job is being trapped without any special trapping zones designated.

TrapWise only traps those intersections that require trapping, ignoring color intersections where trap occurs naturally or is unnecessary. This saves time and improves imaging speed. The program also has special capabilities for trapping gradations, producing a trap line which itself is a gradation to trap the gradations that abut the line.

TrapWise supports keepaway traps by holding back the non-black colors where detailed information is reversed from a rich black. It also supports sophisticated trapping for spot color printing where spot colors trap other spot colors and where they trap process colors.

The Test Squares file opened in Adobe TrapWise, with preview turned on. Through trapping lines are visible—and measurable—in color preview, the trapping lines are more easily viewed when the image is in grayscale mode.

While not able to operate on individual objects, TrapWise allows the operator to define trap zones where different trapping values or techniques can be declared. These zones are limited to rectangular selection areas, but multiple zones can be established simultaneously in a page.

TrapWise uses powerful algorithms for trap color selection that have been fine-tuned through extensive testing in production environments.

Note

An unheralded feature of IslandTrapper and TrapWise is that a service bureau can preview a file before sending it to the imagesetter. A significant percentage of files printed on PostScript machines have some type of problem—a missing graphic, a missing font, or an illustration that won't print. This preview feature allows service bureaus to catch font problems (the number one problem) and other problems before committing a job to expensive film and proofing.

While it would be a relief to dismiss the problems of trapping as solved, it is now, and always will be, important for operators to understand the concepts behind trapping. Even with the advent of sophisticated software trapping software packages, operators will still need to be properly trained in order to derive maximum benefit from these programs.

SCITEX DOLEV IMAGESETTERS

Scitex Corporation, a leader in electronic prepress systems, scanners, and film plotters, has moved into the imagesetting business with a series of PostScript imagesetting systems that have trapping capabilities on a separate workstation.

Based on the technology of its high-end workstations, these imagesetting systems can rasterize PostScript files, convert them into Scitex format, and then perform trapping before output. This technique takes a file from the desktop computer through the rasterizer, then through the bitmapped trapping software, and finally to the film recorder for exposure.

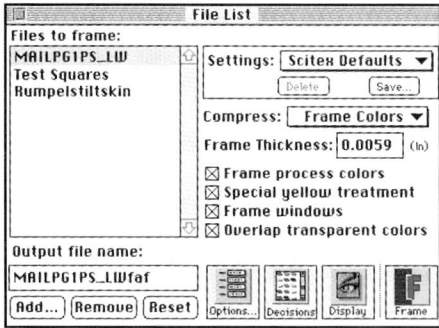

Scitex Full Auto Frames' trapping works on the imagesetter's RIP. The raster-based trapping software is consistently the fastest for trapping PostScript documents in industry evaluations, and yields film that is very satisfactory to printers.

Scitex has applied decades of trapping experience on their high-end prepress systems to this desktop software, bridging the gap between the demand for excellent trapping and the inability of most PostScript graphics applications to deliver it.

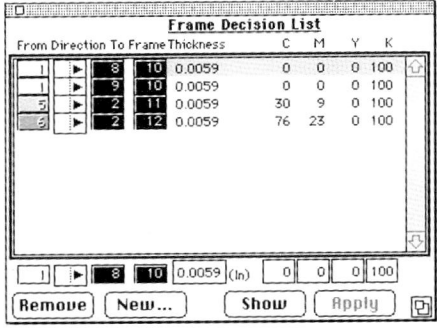

The Full Auto Frames Decision list will list all intersecting colors, indicating the trap colors and their component colors in a job, and allow the operator to modify any one of the colors, the direction of the trap, or its thickness. (Trap line entries in this window are displayed in millimeters.)

Color modifications in Full Auto Frames are global, affecting all similar color intersections in the job.

The trapping capability is built into the RIP for the Dolev-PS imagesetter. The RIP resides on either an IBM compatible or a Power PC-based Macintosh computer. Even with the minimum configuration of the RIP, users can trap jobs that have been rasterized by the RIP.

The trapping program, called Full Auto Frames, allows for either fully automatic trapping or user-controlled trapping. The program automatically detects color edge areas that may require spreading or choking. The trapping file can then be sent out to the Dolev recorders.

Scitex imagesetters offer a successful approach to trapping PostScript documents to produce film that meets the level of quality that is expected of high-end systems.

RAMPAGE RIPS

Rampage Systems builds raster-image processors for imagesetters. Included in the software that runs these RIPs is a complete trapping system called TrapIt. Rampage's trapping takes place in the RIP, after the PostScript file is interpreted and before the film is exposed.

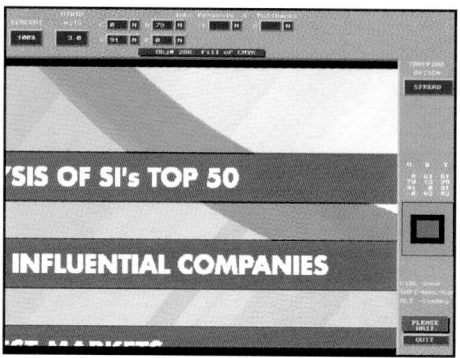

Rampage Systems TrapIt software runs on PC compatibles, and controls the Rampage RIPs. The sophistication of this product goes far beyond the obvious, including the ability to imperceptibly trap shadows and objects made transparent by Rampage's custom Photoshop filter, which can designate objects with clipping paths to have transparent components. Rampage RIP hardware can drive a variety of popular imagesetters from Agfa, Linotype, ECRM, and others.

Rampage trapping software/hardware includes some very impressive features, including the ability to trap multiple transparent objects. Rampage trapping software is competitively fast, and offers complete user-control over every detail of trapping. The RIP even possesses the ability to handle transparent clipping paths on continuous-tone images from Photoshop. By taking advantage of clipping path instructions created with a special Photoshop plug-in called Smart Shadow, the Rampage RIP can treat a drop-shadow as a transparent object, which is subsequently trapped against whatever lies under it.

Rampage RIPs can be purchased to run a variety of popular image-setters from Linotype-Hell, Agfa, Screen, ECRM, and others.

THE NECESSITY OF PROOFREADING

The computer monitor cannot show trapping using current computers and PostScript applications. PostScript treats all colors and all shapes as opaque objects; nothing is transparent in the world of PostScript imaging. Improvements in dye-sublimation proof printers from Du Pont, Radius, and Tektronix, and in ink-jet proof printers like Iris units, allow trapping to be visible in the proof. Changes in the software that drives these printers treats the colors as *separated* colors with overprint transparency; thus trapping lines can be visible in proof prints.

There exists, for the purposes of training and experimentation, an inexpensive method for proofing your work before going to the expense of generating film. This technique is recommended as a test of technique, rather than a method of proofing an entire job, and is not recommended for production because of its slowness and the potential for forgetting to return a trap value to normal before going out to final film.

Most office supply stores sell transparency film sheets (for about $0.75 each) that can be run through a laser printer (make *absolutely* sure that the film is designed for this purpose). These transparency sheets make excellent overheads and overlays. By printing separated pages on a laser printer, and then overlaying these pages, you can easily see if the trapping techniques used will succeed in preventing misregistration.

It is wise when running such tests to increase the amount of trap so that the traps are obvious (even gross) when looking at the final stack of positive transparencies. A four-color page can be proofed in a matter of minutes for a few dollars. If a mistake is found, the savings are tremendous. *Don't forget to return the trap values to their original modest amounts!*

Note

The need for a prepress proof to check your work is essential, and it cannot be omitted from the budget. This kind of shortsightedness will only result in catastrophe. Whenever possible, have the printer or prepress house make a color composite proof (or an overlay proof) of the final film. Look over this proof with a magnifier; make sure all the parts are present and that they trap correctly. Stop the job and rework if needed to repair errors—then proof it again! Even the most confident prepress operator makes at least a blueline proof of the *corrected* job before going to press.

DALIM TRAPPING SYSTEM

Dalim Imaging Software, a German firm, has added a powerful trapping component to the firm's Silicon Graphics-based prepress systems. Working on a file rasterized by the Dalim system, the automatic trapping functions of this program parallel those of the CEPS systems described in the previous chapter by the Dalim system are in PostScript format.

Once created, they are appended to the document, or can be saved independently from the trapped file. Trapping elements can even be printed independently of the original document. Dalim's trapping software considers not only process and spot colors according to their relative luminance, but also metallic colors with special attributes requiring these colors to overprint all others.

The speed of the process roughly equals the fastest hardware systems in the performance of the trapping test files used in the Seybold Report on Electronic Publishing, and exceeds the other software products that performed those tests. The handling of line-ends (PostScript caps and miters) is particularly elegant, with control over not only the miter, but the angle of the miter that is created at the end of a trap element. Individual colors, intersecting objects and groups of objects can be given override values, or be instructed not to trap at all, according to operator instructions. Trapping can also be done automatically with preset trap values and color sets.

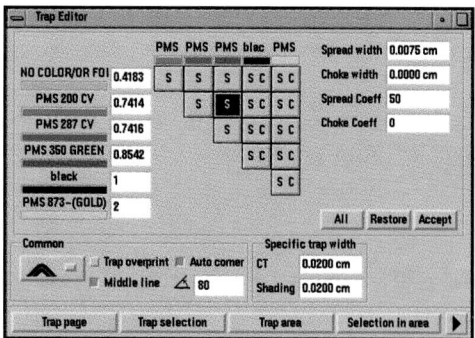

The Dalim trapping system produces vectored trapping graphics that can be appended to any document.

8 The State of the Art of Trapping

PROBLEM: TRAPPING IS A PRODUCTION ISSUE

SOLUTION: ALLOW ADEQUATE TIME FOR TRAPPING

PROBLEM: DESIGNERS DON'T UNDERSTAND TRAPPING

SOLUTION: DELEGATE TRAPPING RESPONSIBILITIES

PROBLEM: IMAGESETTERS AND REGISTER PROBLEMS

SOLUTION: BUILD A RELATIONSHIP WITH THE PRINTING FIRM

PROBLEM: CHANGING PREPRESS ROLES

SOLUTION: TAKE RESPONSIBILITY FOR TRAPPING

Right now, the state of the art of trapping, is rapidly changing—the traditional lithographic trapping process we examined in Chapter 2 has been altered so dramatically that few of the "old ways" still apply. So what's a graphic designer, or a printer, to do about it? To state it briefly, make the necessary changes and roll with them.

This chapter names four significant problems facing the graphic design industry today along with four concurrent solutions. Hopefully these answers, and questions, will help you solve your own trapping dilemmas.

PROBLEM: TRAPPING IS A PRODUCTION ISSUE

Unlike image retouching and color modification, color trapping has no real effect on the aesthetics of a printed job. Trapping, when done correctly, enhances a job's printability, making the task more a production task and less a design task. But, if a designer or publisher is unaware of or uncaring about the need for correct trapping, the project is doomed to mediocrity or even failure.

Solution: Allow adequate time for trapping

Designers and production managers must understand that trapping takes time, and time is money. The important concept here is not only to be aware of the need to trap the job correctly, but also of the need to plan for, budget for, and designate a technique and supplier for getting the trapping done in the course of production.

Also, this is not an unskilled job! Decision-making must take place on every job, because trapping is not an easy or completely automatic process. Even with sophisticated software trapping products, the process requires good judgment, which requires training and experience.

The efficiency of trapping with software or hardware systems is also a factor in productivity. If it takes ten minutes per page to trap a job, and the hourly value of this cost center is $100, the cost of trapping each page is $16.66. This is not an insignificant concern, nor one which should be ignored in planning. If deadlines are tight and trapping must be done, allowances must be made for the time needed to complete the project to appropriate levels of quality.

Most service bureaus, prepress firms, and printers offering trapping as an adjunct service to their customers are charging an hourly or per-page rate for trapping. These charges can add significantly to the cost of production, and must be considered in all budgets and quotations.

PROBLEM: DESIGNERS DON'T UNDERSTAND TRAPPING

One of the most serious color trapping problems is that few designers know how to prepare traps correctly, and many don't understand trapping at all. Graphic arts schools don't teach trapping; even four-year graphic arts programs don't emphasize it in the context of the artist being responsible for the execution of correctly trapping films. It's no coincidence, then, that printers don't get film that traps. This lack of knowledge on the part of designers leads directly to the frustration most printing companies experience when working with designer-provided film.

A central Oregon printer sent two of its employees to a seminar on desktop prepress techniques—one was the chief lithographer, the other a desktop publishing specialist. During the seminar, the lithographer complained that the desktop people never trap their jobs. The desktop publishing specialist said, "What's trap?"

Ironically these two people worked within the walls of the same company, yet they had never exchanged information. The lithographer, with 11 years experience in trapping, was only a few yards away from the people producing the work he was complaining about. They never asked; he never offered. The two went back to work the next day charged with a new assignment: teach each other the tricks of the trade to make a better printed product of each and every job.

Solution: Delegate trapping responsibilities

Ideally, designers should be able to simply design, free of the burdens of technology and the drudgery of detail. But few designers and desktop publishers work in such a situation, so realistic constraints demand realistic solutions.

In some design studios, the process of applying trapping is consciously shifted to a production artist (or a computer trapping workstation) who becomes responsible for making sure that designs are printable. This ensures that one person or a few particular people within a company are always attentive to factors such as color specifications and other trapping concerns. Thus the graphic designer is relieved of responsibility for actually creating traps, without relieving him or her of the responsibility for ensuring that trapping is done.

Either the "designated trappers" within a design firm need to be carefully trained to trap their artwork correctly, or the company should always specify that electronic trapping be done elsewhere.

PROBLEM: IMAGESETTERS AND REGISTER PROBLEMS

Electronic trapping creates some challenges that are different from traditional trapping. This may come as a surprise to most designers and publishers, who for the most part remain blissfully unaware of what happens once their work leaves their hands. Maintaining this level of ignorance, however, is not to your advantage in the long run, especially if you find yourself rushing to meet or beat a deadline and the printer cannot accommodate your needs.

A number of factors contribute to the problem of trapping and fit in prepress projects that involve film created on an imagesetter. First of all, not all imagesetters are accurate, which creates a risk to excellent color production. First-generation imagesetters—such as capstan imagesetters which are roll-fed and roll-exposed—were (and remain) quite inaccurate. While they can be used to set type with quality and speed, the process of color separation is beyond their purpose. At the very best, they are capable of running color separations in small sizes in sequence.

But in the event that a single separation must be rerun, the whole job must be rerun again in sequence. This problem is so bad on some machines that two consecutive pages cannot be produced that will print in register—even the technical manuals for many of these roll-fed machines stress the importance of reprinting a complete set of separations even if only one needs to be replaced.

Solution: Build a relationship with the printing firm

Probably the best investment a graphic arts designer or producer can make is to establish a good working relationship with a printer. If you start building a solid relationship with a printer before you're up against a tight deadline, problems having to do with unknown variables such as tricky imagesetters and registration headaches will be less likely to impact you directly. (Quality relationships are built upon loyalty, flexibility, respect, *and* prompt payment of invoices— not necessarily in that order.)

Wise clients have iron-clad relationships with printing firms that will work overtime or on weekends when a true emergency arises. These wise customers are better planners, better payers, and better customers. They don't buy on price alone, and they don't abandon a printer when a mistake is made.

If trapping problems on either end are causing friction between you and your printer, try communicating directly to solve the problem— your printer is a firsthand source of valuable information, and your misunderstandings may turn out to be easily solved. It is up to you to extract the information and assistance to improve the quality of your printing job, including correct trapping. Don't wait for your printer to offer it.

PROBLEM: CHANGING PREPRESS ROLES

The changes in graphic arts technology over the past few years have shifted much of the responsibility for film preparation onto the shoulders of graphic designers. Traditional graphic arts preparation— the production of paste-ups—was a lowest-common-denominator solution to the reproduction process. Anyone, anywhere could take a paste-up to a printer, and that printer would have been able to print the job; even though the quality of workmanship varied from artist to artist and printer to printer, everyone in the graphic arts industry understood a paste-up and what to do with it.

The art of preparing film for multi-color printing, on the other hand, has always been the domain of the film assembler. Graphic artists, designers, and typographers usually knew little or nothing of the pre-press process; somehow it just happened. Now that electronic pre-press has come of age, the responsibility for managing more detail in the printing process is being passed around. In other words, we all want control over more of the job, and desktop computer technology has accordingly delivered that control.

However, control comes at a price, and that price is responsibility (and liability) for all aspects of the job up to the making of the plate. When designers produce film on a PostScript imagesetter, they become job planners, camera operators, retouching artists, and film assemblers. Wearing all those hats is a risky business even if one possesses adequate trapping skill and knowledge.

Solution: Take responsibility for trapping

Everyone involved in the design and production of artwork for print-ing becomes a business partner in the responsibility for its quality. If the decision is made at the outset to create excellent artwork for printing, then the trapping of that artwork is just one of many steps toward excellence. Once the responsibility for trapping is assigned, the process is relatively easy, and the chances of obtaining a superior printed piece are greater.

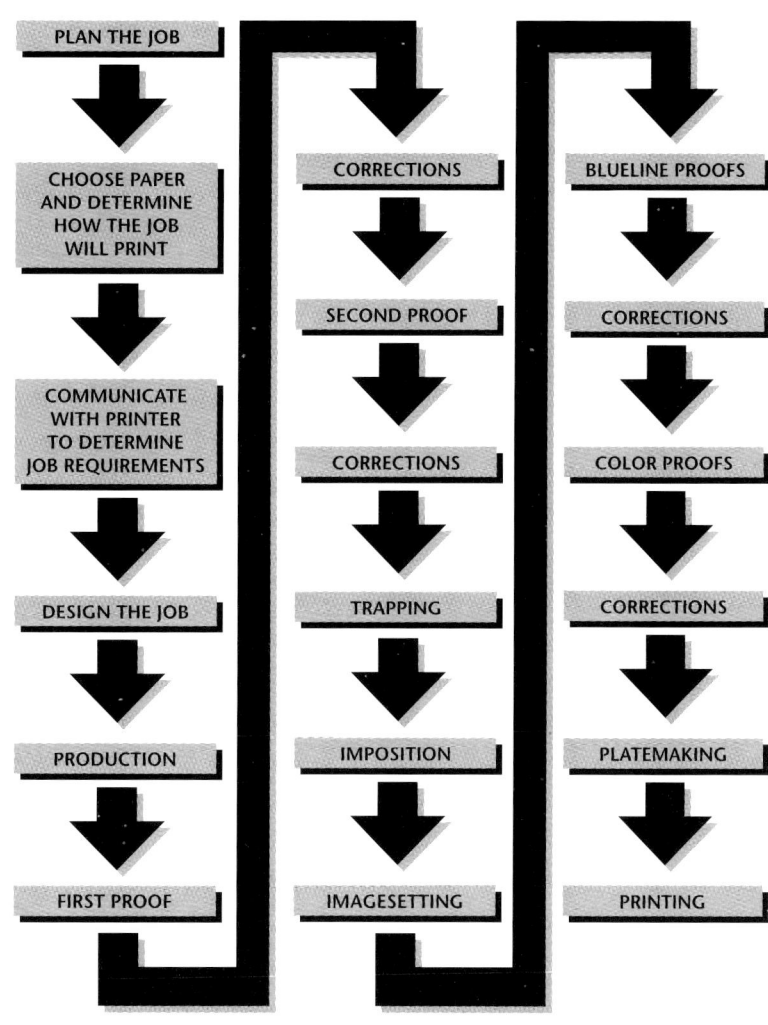

PLAN THE JOB

CHOOSE PAPER AND DETERMINE HOW THE JOB WILL PRINT

COMMUNICATE WITH PRINTER TO DETERMINE JOB REQUIREMENTS

DESIGN THE JOB

PRODUCTION

FIRST PROOF

CORRECTIONS

SECOND PROOF

CORRECTIONS

TRAPPING

IMPOSITION

IMAGESETTING

BLUELINE PROOFS

CORRECTIONS

COLOR PROOFS

CORRECTIONS

PLATEMAKING

PRINTING

9

Workflow Considerations

After reviewing all the technologies, processes, and team members involved in the process of color trapping, it's safe to make the following general observation: There is no single correct method for trapping, just as there is no single procedure for correctly preparing artwork for printing. There is also no single proper distribution of trapping responsibilities, either. The roles of designers and publishers are rapidly changing, as they take on greater control of the prepress function, while printers and service bureaus are forced to react to the moves made by their customers, continually searching for new value-added services to offer.

It's uncertain at this point if designers and publishers will buy into the new generation of trapping software, or if they will continue to look to prepress services to provide digital traps. Either way, today's trapping technology provides designers and publishers with the following options (I recommend this priority):

1. Create conventional mechanicals and allow your printer or prepress house to create conventional film traps.

2. Create digital mechanicals, and allow a suitably experienced printer or prepress house to create electronic film traps.

3. Create digital mechanicals, and handle the trapping yourself using software such as Adobe Illustrator, Macromedia FreeHand, Adobe Photoshop, and QuarkXPress.

4. Use the services of a prepress supplier who uses any of the reliable electronic trapping systems on the market.

5. Create digital mechanicals, and handle the trapping yourself using the new generation of trapping software, such as IslandTrapper or Adobe TrapWise.

While it would be easy to recommend a single workflow scheme, that scheme could not apply in every situation. However complex the issues, by following the chart here it will be possible to develop a production method that will work best for your production circumstances and budget.

On a final note, always remember that every printing project is a custom manufacturing job, and that while one production method may be appropriate to one job, another project will require a completely different approach.

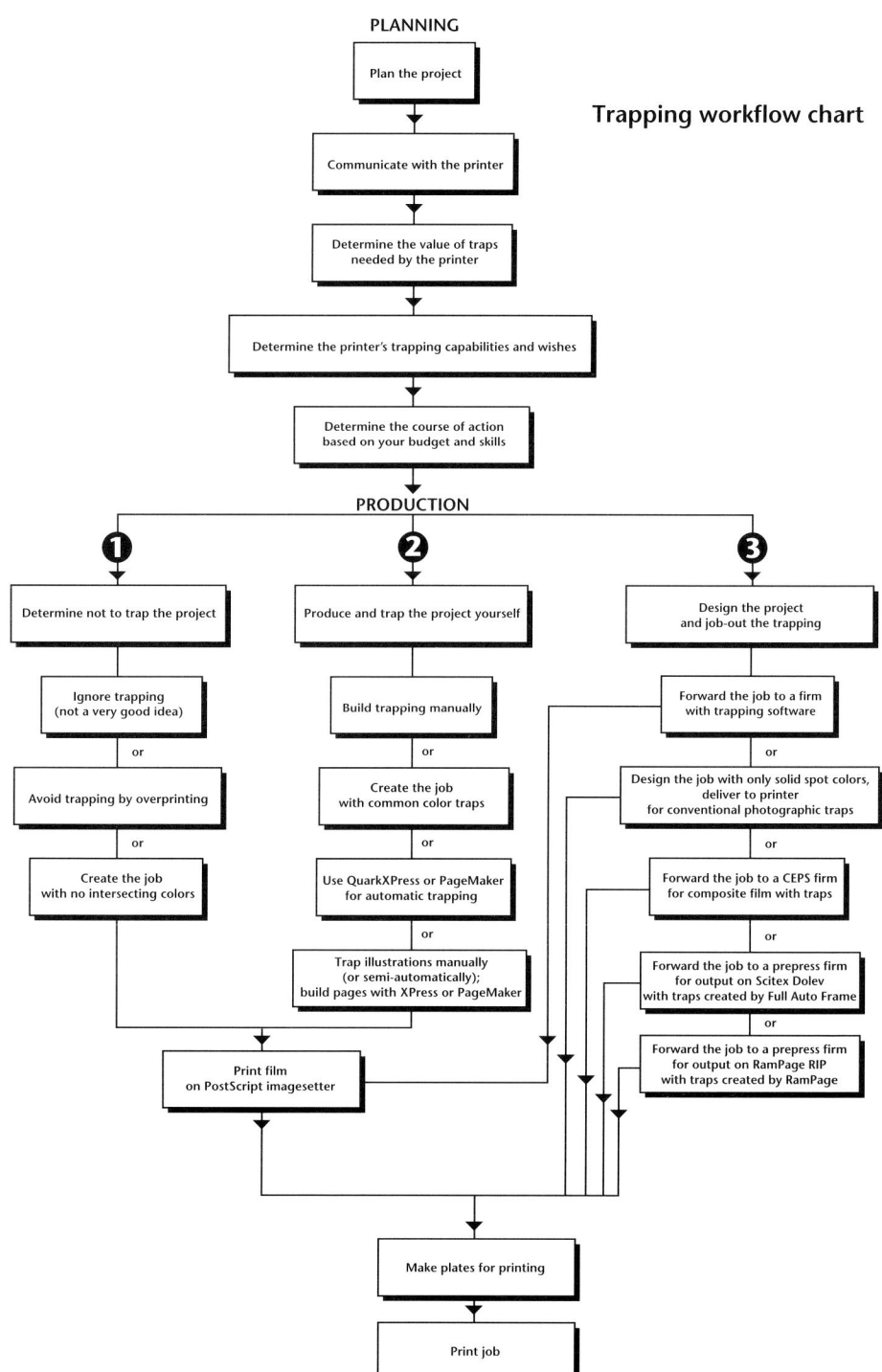

Trapping workflow chart

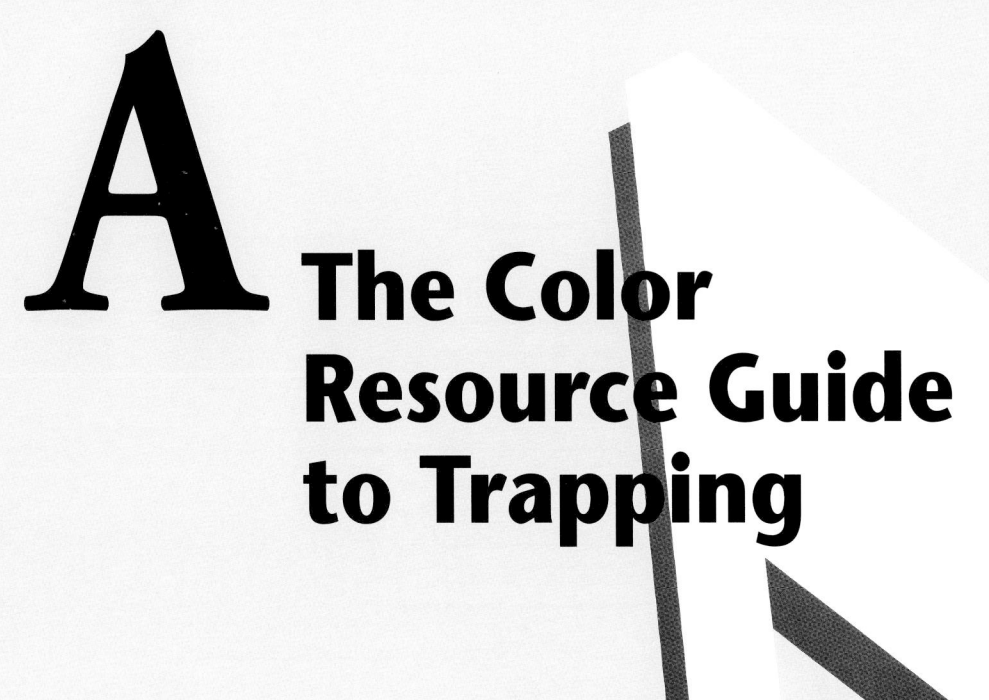

A The Color Resource Guide to Trapping

INTRODUCTION

This Appendix proceeds on the assumption that readers have basic knowledge of trapping and have gone through The Color Resource Trapping tutorial. The information provided here is specific to various Macintosh graphics and page-layout programs: Adobe Illustrator 5.5, Macromedia FreeHand 4.0, QuarkXPress 3.31, Adobe PageMaker 5.0, Adobe TrapMaker 1.0, and Adobe Photoshop 3.0. This Appendix briefly describes the methods of high-end dedicated trapping products such as Adobe TrapWise and IslandTrapper, showing what they have in common and how they differ.

NECESSARY QUESTIONS TO ASK

To create manual traps or to judge automatic traps, it is important to answer the following questions:

When one color touches another, should it be trapped or can it be overprinted?

It is often easier and safer to overprint small objects, such as dark type or rules, than to spread or choke them. When these objects are not so dark, however, overprinting might change their colors. Lighter colors often look muddy when they overprint other colors.

Which of the touching colors is lighter/darker?

It is not always easy to tell which of two colors is lighter or darker. You might wonder if a dark red is darker or lighter than a medium dark blue. As far as 100% colors go, you can rank the CMYK/RGB colors from light to dark in the following way: yellow, cyan, green, magenta, red, blue, black. It becomes more difficult to determine the darkest color when comparing tints or different spot colors such as Pantones. In that case, you could use the following formula to determine the overall lightness of objects. A color's lightness is then determined by: $(30\% \times R) + (59\% \times G) + (11\% \times B)$—R for red, G for green, and B for blue. The higher the outcome of this formula, the lighter the color. The RGB equivalents of Pantone or CMYK colors can be found in most programs' color pickers by choosing the RGB color space to describe the color.

How much spreading or choking is necessary?

There are many existing guidelines for determining the ideal trap width. This issue is so complex because press misregistration depends on a great number of variables—type of paper used, type of presses, humidity, linescreen, the craftsmanship of the press operator, etc. In reality only your printer can give you the answer, so contact him or her before you create your traps.

WARNINGS

Automatic trapping

Never assume that default trap values are the same for each job. Not only could printing variables be different for particular jobs, but individual page elements need to be considered before hitting the automatic trap button. Traps should provide a technical and aesthetically pleasing solution. Sometimes the best solution is to not only spread, but also choke an object—or overprint the object instead of spreading or choking it.

Trapping in multiple programs

Unlike trapping in dedicated programs, such as TrapWise and IslandTrapper, trapping in creative programs requires a multi-step approach. You will have to deal separately with trapping in your drawing packages (such as FreeHand, Illustrator), your photo/paint packages (such as Photoshop), and your page layout packages (such as PageMaker, XPress) if your document contains elements created in these programs. QuarkXPress and PageMaker with TrapMaker have extensive trapping capabilities, but neither can trap within EPS files nor trap EPS files to backgrounds. Most jobs contain EPS elements, which then need to be trapped on an object-by-object basis in Illustrator or FreeHand before placement in page layout programs.

Note also that if you resize the EPS file in XPress or PageMaker, your traps will also be resized. To avoid corrupting your traps, create and trap your file at the correct size in Illustrator or FreeHand before exporting. If you cannot plan the final size beforehand, you will have to go back to the drawing program after resizing in XPress. In the drawing program, you will resize the illustration while keeping the stroke (line) elements the same (choose "preserve line weights" in Illustrator's scaling dialogue box; do not select "lines" in the options of FreeHand's scaling menu). Save the file again as an EPS file, and update it through XPress' Picture Usage dialog box under the Utilities menu. For instance, if you use one logo that was created in Illustrator in five different sizes in XPress, you will have to create five EPS files in Illustrator to assure proper trapping.

PROOFING TRAPS

Be aware that you cannot see traps on your computer screen; all screen colors are opaque (although programs like TrapWise and IslandTrapper can simulate traps on screen). The most secure—and costly—way to check traps is to generate film and post-film proofs such as Matchprints, Cromalins, or Color Keys. Often it is more cost-effective to check traps at an earlier stage. Several prepress proof printers, such as the 3M Rainbow, the Iris, the Radius Proof Positive, and several of the Tektronix printers can display traps in printed proofs.

For desktop publishers who are starting to create their own traps, it is wise to check traps first using cheaper methods. One way is to print black-and-white laser separations on a laser printer and hold them on top of each other over a light source. By printing at the maximum enlargement factor possible in a particular program, you will be able to make sure that traps exist for each object, even though a laser-printer is not the most accurate proofing device. You won't see the resulting trap colors, but at least you can avoid going to film with objects not trapped. An alternative method is to open trapped files or pages in Photoshop (Fig. 1). Make sure that you open the file in CMYK and that anti-aliasing is turned off. By zooming in and using Photoshop's Show Info densitometer, you can see the trap colors and read the CMYK values of the traps.

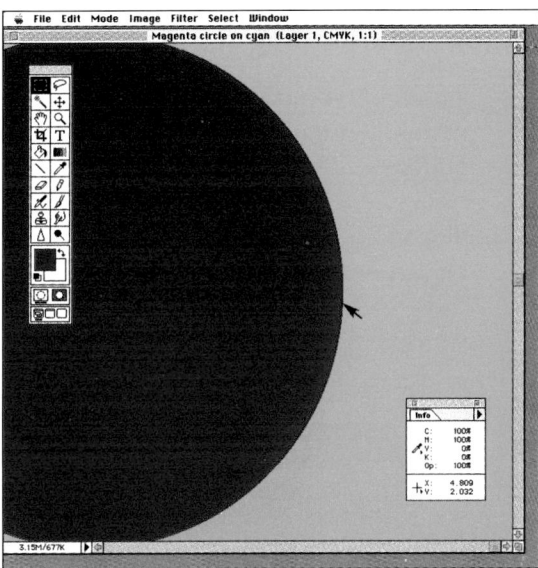

Figure 1

Overprinting black

Not all programs discussed here automatically overprint black text and graphics. This means that you either have to create overprinting fills and strokes for each black object or let black overprint globally. In FreeHand and PageMaker, global overprinting can be achieved in the Print Options dialog box by selecting the black ink and the overprint ink box. Note that global overprinting does not change the information in the file. If someone else prints your file, he or she should use the same procedure. Also, the global overprinting information will not affect printing after files are exported to other programs. A safer approach is to set each individual black element to overprint. Objects set to overprint this way in drawing programs will also overprint when separated out of XPress or PageMaker.

In XPress, black text and black objects overprint by default. This setting can be overridden in XPress' trap information palette. FreeHand and PageMaker overprint black text but knock out black objects by default. Illustrator does not overprint either automatically—black objects nor black text. However, you can create a global overprint of all black elements when separating files using Separator. After you have set all parameters, hold the option key when selecting Save All Separations, Save All Selected Separations, Print All Separations, or Print Selected Separations. This will bring up a message box that asks whether you want to overprint 100% black (Fig. 2).

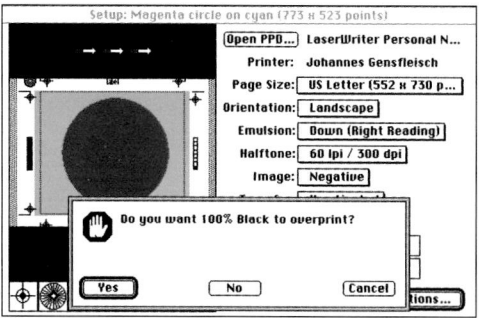

Figure 2

ILLUSTRATOR AND FREEHAND

Until Illustrator 5.5, the basic methods of creating spreads and chokes in Illustrator and FreeHand were similar (Illustrator 5.5 is covered separately in more detail later in this Appendix). Where colors touch, you create an overprinting stroke/line with either the color of the foreground (spread) or the color of the background (choke).

Follow these steps to create traps in Illustrator *and* FreeHand:

- Find areas where colors touch that need trapping (all spot colors—except when you want them to overprint—and all process colors that do not have more than 20% of C, M, Y, or K in common (see more on the use of common colors on the tutorial disk and in Chapter 4).

- Determine which of the touching colors is lighter.

- Select the foreground object, using the arrow tool.

Illustrator

- Open the Paint Style dialog box and mark the box to overprint the stroke. Give it the color of the foreground if this is lighter than the background (spread); give it the color of the background if the background color is lighter (choke). Enter stroke weight. The stroke weight should be twice the desired trap value (Figs. 3 & 4).

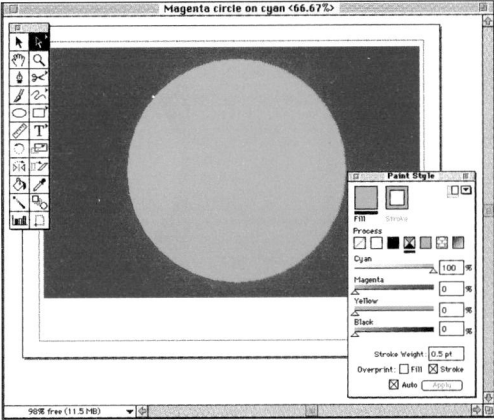

Figure 3

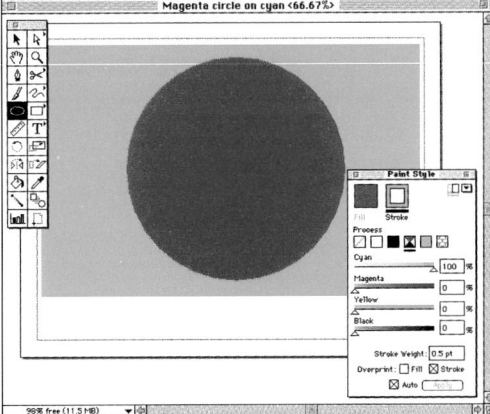

Figure 4

FreeHand

- Open the Attributes Fill and Line dialog box. Select the overprint option for the line. Give it the color of the foreground if this is lighter than the background (spread); give it the color of the background if the background color is lighter (choke). Enter line weight. Remember that the line weight should be twice the desired trap value (Figs. 5 & 6).

- Repeat for all colors that touch.

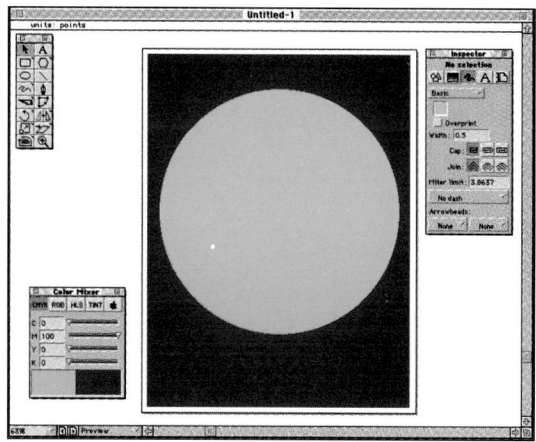

Figure 5

Note

Because the line weight is measured from the center, you will need to double the desired trap value. Half the thickness of the line goes inside the object while the other half goes outside the object. Thus, if you want to spread the overprinting color 0.2 points, you will need to specify 0.4 points for the line weight. See the trapping value chart on page 18 in Chapter 2 for more information on overprinting colors.

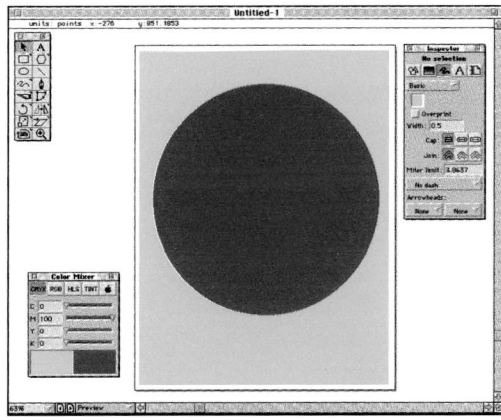

Figure 6

Make sure that when you resize an Illustrator graphic you mark Preserve Stroke Weight in the Scaling dialog box, or when resizing a FreeHand graphic you don't click Lines in the Scaling dialog box. If this is not possible because other strokes in your design would need to be proportionally resized, resize first and redo your traps. Also, keep this in mind when exporting a graphic to a page layout program. If you plan to use the graphic as an EPS file in different sizes, copy the graphic to a new document and resize it as described above. Export each EPS graphic with its own size to your page layout program.

UNDESIRED TRAP COLORS

Neighboring objects in FreeHand and Illustrator that have less than 20% of any process color in common—and, therefore, need to be trapped—might generate distracting trap colors, according to our basic rule of creating overprinting strokes with the colors of the foreground (spreads) or backgrounds (chokes). This is caused by the way PostScript defines overprinting colors. Contrary to what one might think, a 5% magenta stroke that overprints a 100% magenta background creates 5% magenta and not 100% magenta in the overlapping area. A stroke with 1% magenta on top of 100% magenta creates 1% magenta—but an element with 0% magenta in the foreground overprinting a background with 90% magenta generates 90% magenta.

Trap colors are least intrusive if the resulting colors are made up of the highest percentages of cyan, magenta, yellow, and black. For example, a trap with 5% magenta and 100% yellow on top of an object with 100% cyan and 100% magenta, should generate a trap with 100% cyan, 100% magenta, and 100% yellow in the overlapping area. When trapped by the rules we have explained earlier, however, the color in the trapped area would be 100% cyan, 5% magenta, and 100% yellow (Fig. 7). This spread lightens the colors within the darker background, whereas black (100% cyan, 100% magenta, and 100% yellow) in the trapped area would hardly be visible.

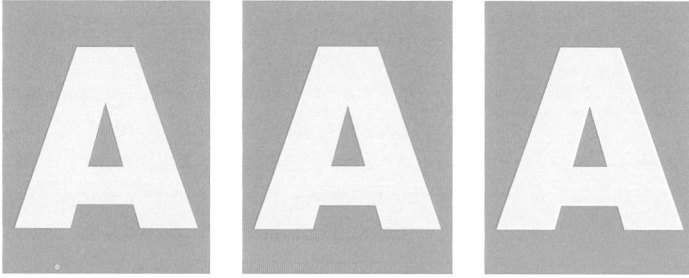

Figure 7

To avoid the artifacts caused by trapping objects with less than 10% in common, you should create overprinting strokes with ink percentages that are the highest in the light colors (thus creating trap colors with the highest percentages of the lightest colors, and the highest percentages of the darkest colors since the ink in the overprinting strokes is set to 0%). For instance, a 5% cyan and 50% magenta object that is spreading onto 70% cyan and 5% magenta needs a trap with 50% magenta only. In Illustrator 5.5, you can lighten the trap through Tint Reduction. For elements created in XPress, choose Process Trap On under the trapping preferences. This triggers Trapping-Per-Plate and avoids undesired trap colors.

Traps depend on availability of strokes
In PostScript, a stroke around an object is considered to be on top of the fill of the same object. It is good to realize that when you don't

assign "overprint" to a stroke, it knocks out its fill (assuming they are not the same color), thus risking white being visible between the fill and the stroke. If you have two different spot colors for the stroke and fill, or process colors that don't have at least 10% in common, you either need to overprint the stroke, or you have to create a trap between the object's fill and its stroke. Let dark strokes overprint when possible.

Blends

Trapping in FreeHand and Illustrator can be cumbersome when graded objects touch gradated backgrounds. The easiest solution is to create a narrow overprinting polygon in the shape of a stroke that blends between the colors. Assign the starting point color that has the highest C, M, Y, and K percentage of the touching colors in this area. For instance, if one neighboring color has 30% cyan, 20% magenta, 40% yellow, and 0% black and the other one has 10% cyan, 40% magenta, 30% yellow, and 10% black, the blend should start with 30% cyan, 40% magenta, 40% yellow, and 10% black. Do the same for the end point of the blended polygon. Although this procedure guarantees optimal traps at these beginning and ending sides, it can lead to poor results in the areas in between. A smoother graded trap can be created in Photoshop through its automatic trapping capabilities (see the Photoshop section later in this Appendix).

FREEHAND SPECIFICS

Strokes as design elements

Objects with colored strokes might need to have the strokes trapped toward the fills. The trap would be too wide if the stroke was simply overprinted. Since the strokes are already used, there are no strokes available to create traps. In FreeHand you can take the following steps to create traps between the objects' strokes and fills (Fig. 8):

- Make a clone of the foreground object, which is automatically placed on top.

- Set the stroke to 0.

- Choose Inset Path (Fig. 9) from Path Operations and choose the trap amount. (Note: You should not double the trap amount here. Note also that in FreeHand a positive amount shrinks an object.)

- Stroke this inset path with double the trap amount and give it the background color if the background is lighter, and the foreground color if the foreground object is lighter.

Outlines

There are situations in which it might be necessary to convert strokes into paths. Outlines that are already used as design elements and need to be trapped cannot be stroked to receive traps. FreeHand 4.0 lets you convert strokes to paths. Once a stroke is converted into a path, an overprinting stroke can be applied as a trap.

FreeHand 4.0 (Fig. 8):

- Select the stroke.

- Apply Arrange-Path Operations-Expand and set the expansion equal to the stroke width. This converts the stroke to an identical path.

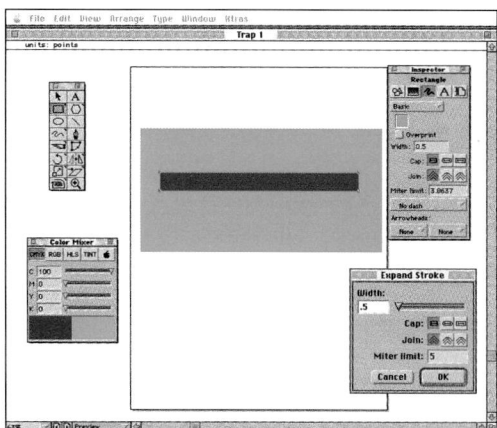

Figure 8

Elements that project across a white background

In FreeHand you can avoid artifacts when trapping elements that partly overlay a background and partly project onto white. An object projecting onto white (partly covering a background object, partly without background) has two problems when traps are applied. When a lighter foreground object spreads, the part that is not touching a background is also expanding because the overprinting stroke around the whole object widens the object. Where the foreground object touches a background, this overprinting stroke creates a trap, which will hardly be noticeable because the trap color will be close to the darker background. However, the object changes shape where the background color ends and the extended overprinting stroke is visible.

In FreeHand 4.0, Arrange and Path Operations let you take the following steps to generate correct spreads when objects project onto white.

- Select the foreground object.

- Make a clone of the foreground object, which is automatically placed on top.

- Apply an overprinting stroke to this clone with double the trap amount and the color of the foreground object's fill.

- Cut this clone.

- Select the background object and apply Paste Inside. Now the background incorporates the overlapping part of the foreground, including an appropriate spread. The original foreground is still visible because it remains on top.

When the top object is darker and partly projecting onto white, a more complicated procedure is necessary. In FreeHand the correct chokes can be made as follows:

- Select both the foreground and the background object.

- Clone them.

- Select the uppermost background and foreground objects.

- Apply Punch under Arrange-Path Operations. This command creates one new shape, subtracting the second highest object from the highest one. In our example, it generates the former background minus the area where the foreground overlapped (Fig. 9 & 10).

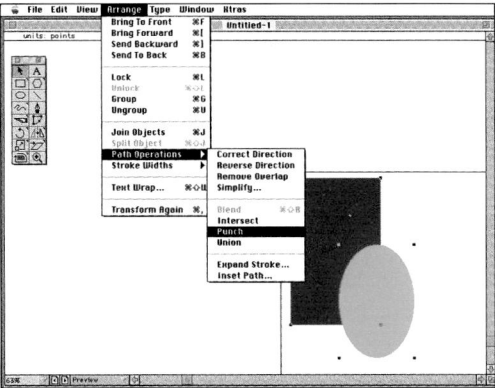

Figure 9

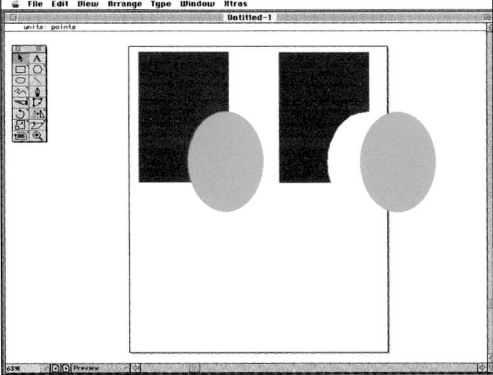

Figure 10

- Place this new shape on a new layer and, for now, turn this layer off because we are going to work with the original foreground and background layer.

- Select the original background object.

- Apply an overprinting stroke with the foreground object's color.

- Copy this background object.

- Select the foreground object.

- Paste the background into the foreground.

- Turn the top layer on and you can see that the punched object guarantees that the overprinting stroke won't be visible within the foreground object.

Note

This method for choking objects that are projecting onto white is more complicated and different from the method described in FreeHand's manual. The simple reason is that FreeHand's method doesn't work. Also keep in mind that Illustrator 5.5 automatically lets you trap only where objects touch.

ILLUSTRATOR SPECIFICS

The arrival of Illustrator 5.5 has made trapping substantially easier. The program no longer requires that users create overprinting strokes or make special provisions for indeterminate traps, objects projecting onto white, and objects that already use strokes as design elements. It also offers control over the trap colors.

You can set traps through Illustrator's new Pathfinder Trap filter as follows:

- Select two or more objects to be trapped (make sure the objects are not overprinting, otherwise you get a message that the filter added no traps to the selected artwork).

- Choose Pathfinder-Trap and enter the values in the Trap dialog box (Fig. 11 & 12).

- Thickness is the actual trap width. Do not double this amount, as was necessary in earlier versions when creating traps through overprinting strokes.

- Height/width allows you to compensate for paper stretching in a particular direction. Check with your printer if that is likely to be the case with your print job. 100% height/width means that the traps compensate evenly for possible misregistration. 80% height/width indicates that the trap will be proportionally thicker in the horizontal direction. 120% means that the trap will be 20% thicker in the vertical direction.

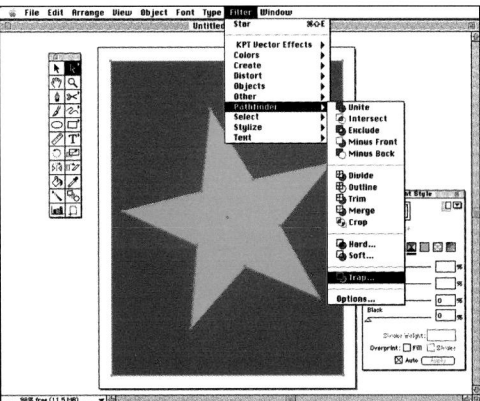

Figure 11

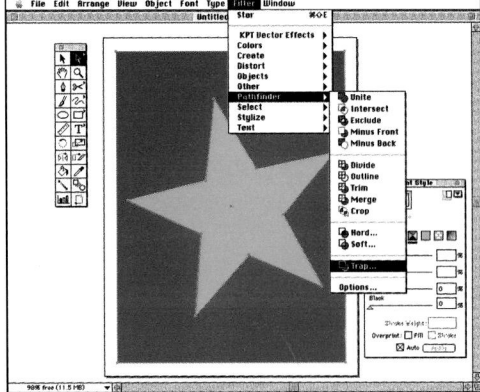

Figure 12

- Tint Reduction is a way to avoid traps that are too dark. This can happen when certain light colors overprint others. The default of 100% means that the resulting trap color is not reduced. 80% means that the overprinting CMYK values of the lighter color are reduced to 80% of their value when overprinting the darker color. The darker object's CMYK colors will be unchanged, but the resulting trap color is lighter because a lighter trap is overprinting the background with unchanged darkness.

- Convert Custom Colors to Process means that the trap color is a process color when one of the neighboring objects has a custom color (such as a Pantone color) and the adjacent object is a process color. The actual process trap color is based on the program's knowledge of the CMYK equivalents of the custom color.

- When Convert Custom Colors to Process is not selected, the trap will be the custom color if the custom color is lighter, or it will be the process color if that color is lighter.

- Reverse Trap is an option to have the darker object spread into the lighter one, instead of spreading the lighter object.

Objects with strokes can also be trapped with this procedure, if you first convert the object's stroke into a path:

- Select the object.

- Select Filter-Objects-Outline path. This changes the strokes into paths (objects).

- Then, select the objects to be trapped and follow the procedure outlined above.

Illustrator 5.5's trap filter also deals effectively with indeterminate backgrounds and foreground objects projecting onto white, since the program creates traps only where objects touch.

Type can be trapped when first converted to outline text. Note that trapping a large amount of colored type can take a long time to process and print. In general, overprinting type is advisable for dark text. If you are uncertain about the resulting color of the type, you can get a quick idea by opening the Illustrator file in Photoshop or making a film proof of a test area of your file.

Unlike traps in XPress, Illustrator's traps are new objects in your file that you can manipulate if desired. All trapped objects are grouped. For further manipulation, it is advisable to immediately place them on a new layer. After ungrouping, you can create different colors for particular traps. Make sure that you base the new color values on your estimate of what the overprinting color combination will look like, and don't base it on how the color appears on your screen.

When resizing the objects after traps are made, the trap size will change. Before resizing, delete the traps and make traps again after resizing. You can automatically trap the whole page, or you can trap per object pair. When trapping the whole page, be aware that colored text and objects with colored strokes need to be converted to outlines and paths respectively, before traps can be made.

AUTOMATIC TRAPPING IN PHOTOSHOP

Photoshop's automatic trapping allows for creating spreads and chokes in bitmapped files. You can only access this trapping option if you convert your file to CMYK. Be aware that continuous tone photographs don't require trapping. Although misregistration of CMYK plates might create some blurriness in the picture, trapped pictures will look worse. Normally only the edges of the picture need correction because one or more colors might be visible. You can do this by creating a frame that overprints the edge of the picture in your drawing or page layout program.

Trapping in Photoshop is very useful when used in conjunction with the program's blending tool. You can create your blends as continuous tones in Photoshop, trap them and save the files as EPS files before exporting to Illustrator or FreeHand. Since Photoshop works with bitmapped data (as opposed to vector-described data in the drawing and page layout programs), each area where different colors touch is analyzed and adjusted by assigning CMYK values that create overprinting colors. This way, each point in the touching area between two blends is analyzed and automatically assigned a trap color rather than only the beginning and ending points, as is the case with traps of blends in Illustrator and FreeHand. Photoshop 3.0 can either trap the entire image, or a selected area.

PAGEMAKER SPECIFICS

Until recently, trapping in PageMaker was complicated and required the user to create manual traps. With the PageMaker Addition, TrapMaker, users can now create traps automatically. Like QuarkXPress, the program's automatic spreading and choking decisions are based on a comparison of the darkness values of neighboring objects (neutral density comparison). The program supports keep aways for rich blacks. It also only traps elements created in the page layout program but does not trap imported EPS files.

TrapMaker lets the users edit default settings. Edit trapping defaults for specific color combinations in "Overrides" (similar to XPress' Edit Color - Edit Trap semi-automatic trap settings). The program does not let the user change trap width values for individual objects like in XPress' trap palette, but users can work around this limitation by defining custom colors with names that are only used for objects that need special trap settings (such as when plate green is the foreground over table brown).

TrapMaker does not automatically save a file's trap settings with the file. Instead, it automatically generates a separate .tm file in the same folder as the publication each time the user opens TrapMaker and closes out of it by clicking the done button. If a service bureau also uses TrapMaker, they can apply these settings when outputting if the .tm file is in the publication's folder.

The program's strength is its ability to create trap lines only where colors touch (instead of creating overprinting strokes around entire objects, as is the case in XPress). This means that objects that are partially projecting on white will get a trap where they touch other objects, but they won't expand where there is no colored background. This way PageMaker with TrapMaker has a solution for "indeterminate trapping" (compare with the QuarkXPress section). TrapMaker has the unique ability to assign spreads, chokes, and centerline traps in cases where the objects have a similar darkness. Thus, neither object will look like it is expanded or shrunk by the entire trap amount. TrapMaker can also automatically apply wider traps to colors that touch solid black objects. Finally, a step limit option determines when TrapMaker needs to create traps between objects with common color ingredients.

Another PageMaker Addition, Create Keyline, offers precise control over how edges of imported images can be trapped to any background (Fig. 13 & 14).

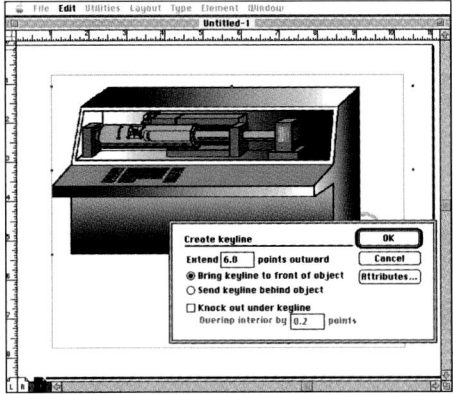

Figure 13

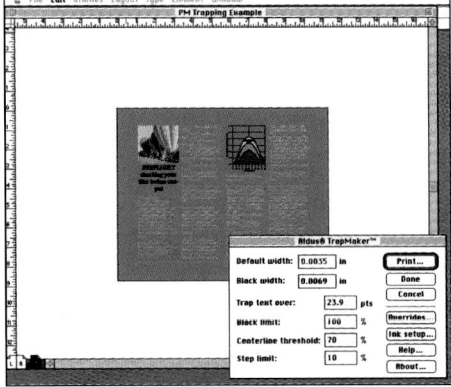

Figure 14

When an image has no background, you can make sure that no fringes of cyan, magenta, yellow, or black will be visible on the edges by creating an overprinting black keyline. When there is a colored background, the keyline should have the color of the background:

- Select the image.

- Additions-Create keyline.

- Extend Points Outward: Fill in the trap amount; select Bring keyline in front of objects; Attributes: Line width: two times the trap amount; line should be set to overprint.

QUARKXPRESS

XPress 3.31 allows the user to trap automatically, semi-automatically, and on an object-by-object basis. As opposed to Illustrator and FreeHand, XPress analyzes the brightness of the objects and decides accordingly whether to spread or choke the foreground objects. You don't have to worry about which color is darker and which is lighter, and you also don't have to select each individual object to create spreads or chokes. As with the drawing packages, you need to decide on the trapping values (how much to spread or choke), although XPress comes with default values in the application preferences. Be aware that even when you don't hit any trapping button and you go to print, you have automatically used these default trapping values. Also, make sure that the default settings are correct for the type of print job you are doing (check with your printer). As an example, if you plan to print on lower quality paper, you need larger trap values than when printing on quality coated stock. Make sure the automatic trapping values are correct for the design elements you have created. Finally, as mentioned earlier, be aware that EPS files cannot be trapped in XPress; they need to be trapped in Illustrator or FreeHand.

XPress' default settings can be overridden on three different levels:

- On a global scale by choosing a different Auto Amount in the Application Preferences menu (Automatic Trapping)

- On a per color basis by choosing Edit Trap under the Edit Color menu (semi-automatic trapping)

- On a per object basis by selecting the object and replacing the default trap values by custom trap values for the foreground color (Object Trapping)

Automatic Trapping in XPress

QuarkXPress has a default trapping amount that is set in the Application Preferences menu. The program comes with a default amount of .144 points. Unless you change this, each color you use (with the exception of black) is trapped with .144 points. Once you change the default value, this new amount will become the default in all files you create *only if* there are no documents open. Otherwise, you have changed the default settings only in the one file you're working on. As explained in the tutorial disk, the correct trapping amount is crucial to proper trapping and depends on many press-room variables. Never assume that XPress' default setting, or your self-created default trap amount, is the amount that will work with every print job. For each job, consult your printer as to whether to retain or adjust this amount.

Note

QuarkXPress, beginning with version 3.1, saves Application Preferences with each document. Therefore it is critical that when someone else opens your file, they must choose the option for keeping the existing document preferences, rather than opening it with their own.

XPress' default trapping choices also include Overprint Limit, meaning that with a default value of 95% all shades of 95% black or darker will automatically overprint background colors, instead of being choked by these backgrounds.

The default of Indeterminate Trapping refers to situations where one foreground color is on top of at least one lighter and one darker background color. XPress cannot spread an object where it touches a darker background and choke it where it touches a lighter background. Instead, it lets users choose whether they want no trapping at all (knocking out, i.e. 0 pt. trap), or a certain spread or choke value that applies to all edges of the foreground objects. As explained earlier, be aware that when very dark colors spread or choke, trapping might corrupt the image. One solution we recommend in this situation is using common colors to eliminate the need for trapping altogether. This method is covered in more detail in Chapter 4, "How to Avoid Trapping."

Ignore White refers to your choice of having XPress ignore white background colors when analyzing the required trap for a foreground color that partly overlaps a background color and partly abuts a paper background. With Ignore White selected, the default trap value will be chosen; if it is not selected the indeterminate value will be chosen because the white background will be considered the second background color. In most cases, the Ignore White default value is preferable to indeterminate trapping values.

Process Trap refers to XPress' ability to analyze a foreground object and create separate spreads or chokes on the C, M, Y, and K plates, according to the differences in darkness between the foreground and background color. Instead of analyzing the foreground color and giving an overall spread or choke to this object, Process Trap minimizes visual distortion by doing the same comparison per C, M, Y, and K plate. This may result in one object being choked on some plates and being spread on others, based on differences in lightness between individual plates.

Semi-automatic trapping in QuarkXPress

If necessary, you can change the default trapping settings of a particular color by choosing Edit Trap for the color in XPress' Color box under the Edit menu. From there you can change the values for each occasion that the selected foreground color will be trapped against specific background colors. As an example, you can change the trap relation between green as a foreground and red as a background color. This change will override the default trap settings. (Fig. 15)

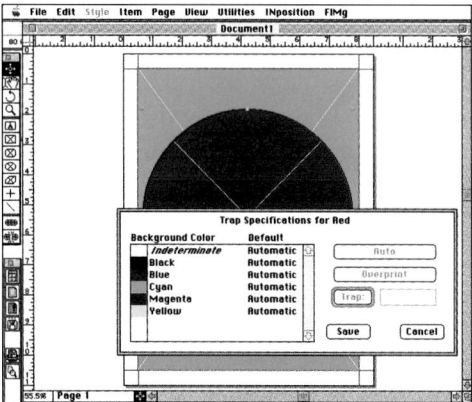

Figure 15

Object trapping in QuarkXPress

Automatic and semi-automatic trapping values can be overridden by assigning different trap values to selected foreground objects. In XPress' trapping palette (which can be selected through View-Show Trap Information) you have the choice of changing the default value into Knockout, Overprint, Auto Amount (+), Auto Amount (–), or Custom values. Auto amount (+) and auto amount (–) will change chokes into spreads and vice versa. You can also accomplish this in the Custom option where you can type a + or a – in front of the default value. This custom option is also the place to assign a trapping amount to a particular object that is different from the default amount (Fig. 16).

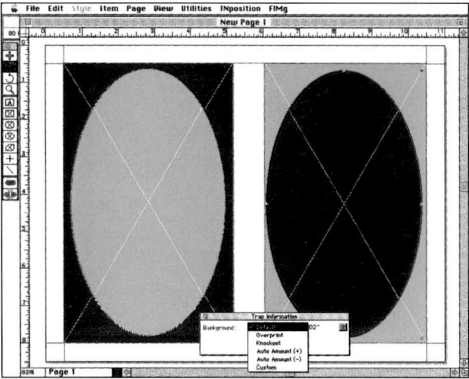

Figure 16

When using the trapping palette, you can also see (and override if desired) how XPress allows frames of graphic and text boxes to trap. When selecting the foreground object, you can see that the frame of a graphic box can be trapped differently inside (into the box's background) from outside (into another background).

Text can be spread into its text box's background, whereas the text box itself is choked by another background.

Note that an imported EPS graphic cannot be spread or choked into the graphic box's background color. If you need to trap your EPS graphic into a background color, it is necessary to include the background in your EPS file and trap it in your Illustrator or FreeHand source file. Alternatively, you can assign an overprinting stroke with double the trap amount and either the object's color (for spreads) or the same color for chokes as later will be used in XPress for the background.

Also note that the trapping settings of XPress' frames are related to the box's background and not the EPS that was placed in the box. If the EPS is so large that XPress' background does not show, the frame overprints this EPS graphic. Overprinting in this case means overprinting with the inner half of the frame's width. You can overrule this default overprinting by selecting custom spread or choke values, but in most cases (dark, narrow frames) this type of overprinting works fine.

XPRESS SPECIFICS

Rich blacks

Blacks that contain percentages of other CMYK colors are automatically kept away when they border white areas, such as the paper background or reversed text. This procedure chokes the cyan, magenta, and yellow colors to prevent them from being visible as small fringes in the white areas surrounding the black.

Small objects and type

Small objects (with dimensions equal to or smaller than 10 points in diameter) and type (24 points or smaller) could in rare instances fail to trap. This situation occurs only with process trap on. XPress does not trap these elements when, per process color, the foreground object's tint percentage is half the darkness or less than that of its background for the same process color. If this happens with all four process colors, a trap will be missing. Always check your film, because XPress' trap information palette doesn't warn you about this.

XPress EPS pages

Pages saved in XPress as EPS pages will lose all trapping information. This is not the case with XPress documents printed to disk.

Choking type on top of an indeterminate background

Due to a limitation in PostScript, it is impossible to choke type by an indeterminate background. The trap palette does not let you change its value to choke.

SXetchPad

The SXetchPad XTension lets XPress users make drawings in XPress. Drawings generated this way are automatically trapped like any other element created in XPress, and it saves users some of the hassles of creating complicated traps in FreeHand and Illustrator.

Objects covering bitmapped images

Bitmapped images, such as imported photos from Photoshop, can be illustrated in XPress with headlines or drawings. By default, headlines or XPress drawings will be trapped with indeterminate trap amounts. The user can only spread the headline over an indeterminate background that cannot be choked. (Fig. 17)

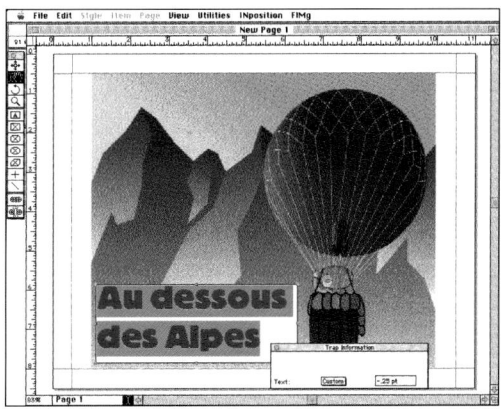

Figure 17

DEDICATED TRAPPING PROGRAMS

Dedicated trapping programs are specifically made to be used as a production tool, usually by prepress production or printing facilities. Some require a file to be rasterized on a specific raster image processor (such as Scitex Full Auto Frames), others rasterize or convert the files through software, independent of any RIP. Dedicated trapping programs are more productive in creating traps than creative graphics programs because they take file information out of the PostScript mode into either rasterized data (such as Scitex Full Auto Frame or Adobe TrapWise) or into a proprietary vector description language (IslandTrapper). This way, all the necessary traps can be created in just one program. In order to not create traps on traps it is important that no previous traps were made in the drawing or page layout programs.

Rasterizing programs have the advantage that the programs' decisions whether to spread or choke toward blends or bitmapped images are based on the actual pixel color data of the page elements. IslandTrapper only allows users to have all elements either spread or choke toward blends or images, independent of actual color values, because the program cannot convert this data of the original files to its vector language.

For production facilities, workflow is a key factor. Programs like Scitex Full Auto Frames had the advantage of needing to RIP the files only once (the rasterized file is then trapped and ready to output to film). TrapWise (Fig. 18) needs to RIP the file once in order to generate a trappable file, but before film output, it again needs to RIP the file using the imagesetter RIP. Version 2.0 brought the advantage that the user can at least print separations directly out of TrapWise, instead of exporting the trapped EPS files to other programs for film output.

The last workflow is required by IslandTrapper (Fig 19) because the program lacks separation capabilities. IslandTrapper needs to convert the file once in order to make traps. The trapped file then needs to be saved as an EPS, which is then exported to a page-layout or separation program where it is processed by the imagesetter RIP.

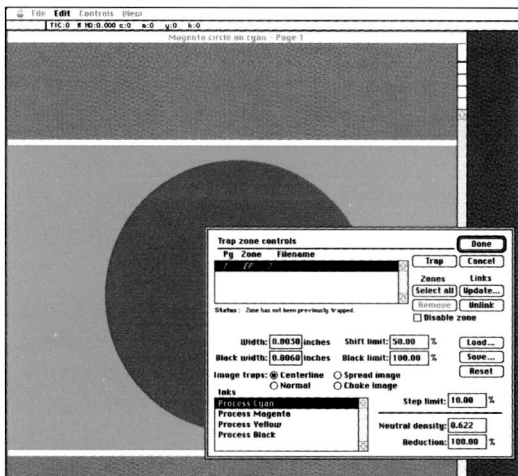

Figure 18

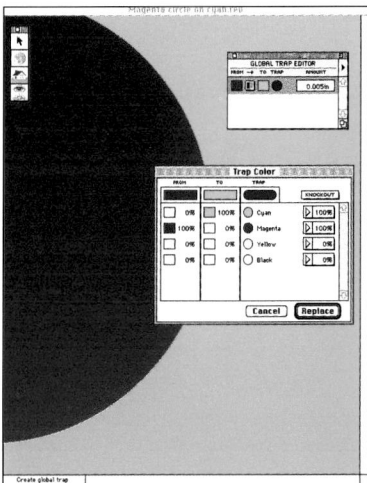

Figure 19

It is unclear whether, or to what extent, services using dedicated trapping programs are going to replace trapping in graphics programs. With certain applications suffering from a complicated workflow, some service providers have found it to be more productive to do the required manual traps in Illustrator or FreeHand and let the page layout program handle the remaining traps. Others, especially more complicated files, can be trapped faster in Scitex Full Auto Frames, TrapWise, or IslandTrapper. If there is any consensus, it is that even with automated trapping tools, the quality of the traps depends on the user's production knowledge.

B

Vendor List

Adobe Systems, Inc.
P.O. Box 7900
Mountain View, CA 94039-7900
415/962-2000

Agfa (Miles, Inc.)
200 Ballardvale Street
Wilmington, MA 01887
508/658-5600

Barco, Inc.
1000 Cobb Place Boulevard
Kennesaw, GA 30144
404/590-7900
FAX 404/590-8042

Dalim Imaging Software
Bedford Executive Office Park
Two Executive Park Drive
Bedford, NH 03110
603 624-5994

DuPont Imaging Systems
65 Harristown Road
Glen Rock, NJ 07452-3393
201/447-5800

InSight Systems, Inc.
10017 Coach Road
Vienna, VA 22182
703/938-0250

Iris Graphics
Six Crosby Drive
Bedford, MA 01730
617/275-8777

Island Graphics Corporation
4000 Civic Center Drive
San Rafael, CA 94903
415/491-1000

Linotype-Hell Company
425 Oser Avenue
Hauppauge, NY 11788
516/434-2000

Professional Computer Center
23 Summit Square
Langhorne, PA 19047
215/860-5200
FAX 215/860-2646

Purup North America
1326 Energy Park Drive
St. Paul, MN 55108-5202
612/646-3388
FAX 612/646-7832

Quark, Inc.
1800 Grant Street
Denver, CO 80203
303/894-8888

Rampage Systems, Inc.
63 Third Avenue
Burlington, MA 01803
617/891-9800

Scitex America Corporation
Eight Oak Park Drive
Bedford, MA 01730
617/275-5150

Screen U.S.A. Inc.
>5110 Tollview Drive
>Rolling Meadows, IL 60008
>708/870-1960

Utility Company
>2775 Mesa Verde East, Suite X105
>Costa Mesa, CA 92626
>714/754-1087

Varityper, A Tegra Company
>11 Mt. Pleasant Avenue
>East Hanover, NJ 07936-2688
>201/887-8000

Ventura Software, Inc.
>1600 Carling Avenue
>Ottawa, Ontario K1Z8R7
>CANADA
>613/728-8200

Xyvision
>101 Edgewater Drive
>Wakefield, MA 01880-1291
>617/245-4100

C Bibliography

Adobe Systems, Incorporated. *Adobe Photoshop Users Guide.* Mountain View, CA: Adobe Systems, Incorporated, 1994.

Beach, Mark. *Graphically Speaking.* Manzanita, OR: Elk Ridge Publishing, 1992.

Blair, Ray and Thomas Destree, eds. *The Lithographer's Manual,* Ninth Edition. Pittsburgh, PA: Graphic Arts Technical Foundation, 1994.

Bruno, Michael, ed. *Pocket Pal, A Graphic Arts Production Handbook,* Fifteenth Edition. Memphis, TN: International Paper Company, 1992.

Cardamone, Tom. *Mechanical Color Separation Skills for the Commercial Artist.* New York, NY: Van Nostrand Reinhold Company, 1980.

Cozart, Jerry. *Film Contacting (Making Spreads and Chokes).* Pittsburgh, PA: Graphic Arts Technical Foundation, 1980.

Groff, Pamela J., ed. *GATF Glossary of Graphic Arts Terms.* Pittsburgh, PA: Graphic Arts Technical Foundation, 1991.

Myrick, Jim and Hans Hartman. *Trapping* (disk and booklet). San Francisco, CA: Pixel Ink Consultants, 1991. Revised 1994, now published by The Color Resource, San Francisco, CA.

Peck, Harold L. *Stripping: The Assembly of Film Images,* Second Edition. Pittsburgh, PA: Graphic Arts Technical Foundation, 1988.

Southworth, Miles; Thad McIlroy, and Donna Southworth. *The Color Resource Complete Color Glossary.* Livonia, NY: The Color Resource, 1992.

G Glossary

art boards   See *paste-ups*.

bitmap   A graphic image consisting of many tiny cells of numerical computer data. The number of cells determines the resolution of the bitmap, while the value of each cell establishes the density or darkness of each cell—therefore its tone. Photographic information is stored in a computer in bitmap form. Full-color photos are stored as large multi-layer bitmap images whose cells have numerical information stored for tone and color.

bridge color   See *common color*.

butt-fit   When two or more objects print immediately adjacent to one another, and no attempt is made to create an overlapping trap of the subordinate color or tone, what remains is a butt-fit. Left alone, all PostScript imagesetters will print adjacent colors as butt-fits, no allowance being made for trapping. Also known as *kiss-fit*.

capstan imagesetter   Along with drum imagesetters, this is one of the two main classes of imagesetters. Capstan imagesetters are roll-fed imagesetters that image with a laser beam onto a section of a continuous roll of material. The term capstan refers to a three-element design consisting of a single capstan roller and two sets of pinch rollers that keep the material taut on the capstan. Most of these machines are inadequate for high-precision color imagesetting, though recent advances in technology have advanced the state-of-the-art. See also *drum imagesetter*.

CEPS   Abbreviation for **C**olor **E**lectronic **P**repress **S**ystems. These are dedicated computer systems for scanning, managing, retouching, adjusting, and composing photographic and graphic elements. Manufactured primarily by four firms, these CEPS operations are often known by their trade names: Scitex, Du Pont (Crosfield) Studio, Screen Sigmagraph, and Linotype-Hell ChromaCom. These highly sophisticated systems can manipulate color images, assemble pages, trap all colors and prepare composite film—ready for plate.

choke   The opposite of *spread*, an image that is choked is usually contacted from the original film positive in a vacuum frame onto a new sheet of film with a clear layer of film in between. Diffused light undercuts the image, reducing the size of the resulting duplicate. The choke is used to make a trap with an unmodified second color. Also known as *crimp*, *shrink*, *skinny*, and *squeeze*.

common color   A color that is a component of two other different colors, added to existing colors in a design to eliminate or reduce the potential of misregistration. For example, yellow is common to red (yellow + magenta) and green (yellow + cyan). Usually 20 percent of common color is the minimum requirement. Also known as *bridge color*.

Control Panel   The Control Panel is a Macintosh software window that gives the user access to controls that affect the computer's basic functions. The number of colors displayed on the screen, or the speed of response to the mouse can be changed here. Controls for networking, file sharing, memory management, and others are all accessed through the Control Panels window.

crimp   See *choke*.

CMYK   Abbreviation for **C**yan, **M**agenta, **Y**ellow, and Blac**k**, the four process colors.

default   Most computer software comes from the publisher with certain functions established by the authors. These settings are called "default" settings because they are the most basic controls for that product. Overriding the defaults, or changing them permanently, is a common procedure.

display type   Usually defined as type set at 24 point or larger, display type is usually used for headlines or banner information. In terms of trapping, display type—as long as it is bold enough to withstand the rigors of trapping—can be treated just like any other graphic element. Delicate typefaces with extremely thin elements are not suitable for certain trapping techniques, and must be treated by exception rather than rule.

dots-per-inch (dpi)   Usually used to measure scanner or printer resolution, the *dot-per-inch* has become another confusing element in the list of units-of-meaure in the electronic graphic arts industries. Often a device such as a scanner will request a value for resolution to be entered in *dpi*. See also *lines-per-inch* and *pixels-per-inch*.

drum imagesetter   The two main classes of imagesetters are capstan and drum. Drum imagesetters, which fall into two sub-classes, expose material in or around a drum. These machines are typically more precise and more capable of repeatable work because the film remains stationary during exposure, and the machines are generally built to more exacting standards. Internal drum machines expose film in a continuous roll that is held stationary inside a trough. External drum machines are sheet-fed, and expose the film as it rotates on the drum. Both types of devices are capable of very high quality output. See also *capstan imagesetter*.

drum scanner   A drum scanner scans an original image (either reflective or transparent) that has been wrapped around its transparent plastic drum. Drum scanners are traditionally the best available. Several major manufacturers produce excellent drum scanners, among them are Linotype-Hell, Screen, and Du Pont Imaging Systems (Crosfield).

dry trapping   The discussion of how one ink layer adheres to another ink layer that is already dry. Inks are formulated to create a dry surface that will allow subsequent ink layers to be overprinted with good adhesion. Also known as *wet trapping*.

EPS   Abbreviation for Encapsulated PostScript, a file type that is created by a wide variety of computer programs. EPS files contain all of the vector and bitmap information necessary to image a single page. These files are usually not intended to be printed by themselves, but they are placed in a page design and then printed. The term EPSF is the same thing—the F stands for file.

EPS files are used by most graphics and drawing programs because they can be modified by a subsequent operation (scaled, rotated, distorted, mirrored, etc.) without any damage to their quality. One should be careful with EPS files that contain bitmapped graphics (photos or other continuous-tone images). Bitmapped graphics can be stored in EPS format, but they are not as tolerant of subsequent modification.

fatty   See *spread*.

flat   An assemblage of film, taped to a carrier sheet and positioned ready for exposure to a printing plate. Though usually comprised of multiple pages, a flat describes any film made ready for such exposure.

flexography   A printing process that uses flexible relief plates made of rubber or photopolymer materials. Flexographic printing accounts for the majority of food product labels and packaging, and represents one of the largest dollar-volume portions of the printing industry as a whole. Its benefits include the ability to print on plastics, rough and thick substrates including corrugated board, and its ability to print with non-toxic inks.

GATF   The **G**raphic **A**rts **T**echnical **F**oundation, a Pittsburgh, Pennsylvania-based graphic arts industry research and training organization.

grip   See *trapping*.

hairline register   The process of printing with no intentional trapping. This is very difficult and very costly printing, and occurs rarely. In many cases, due to the condition of printing machinery or preparation techniques, it may be impossible to achieve. Trapping eliminates the need for hairline register printing.

halftone frequency   A measurement of the count of halftone dots in a linear inch or centimeter. Greater frequency means smoother tones, and less contrast. See also *dots-per-inch*.

hold back   See *keepaways*.

image assembly   See *stripping*.

imagesetter   A laser imaging device for recording a page of information on photographic or plain paper at reproduction quality. PostScript imagesetters are the most commonly used, producing photographic paper or film images for subsequent reproduction on printing presses. Usually the images made by these devices are drawn by a laser beam that is modulated by a liquid-crystal shutter and deflected by a rotating mirror or prism. The laser is programmed by a computer called a RIP (**R**aster **I**mage **P**rocessor). See also *capstan imagesetter, drum imagesetter,* and *RIP*.

ink trapping   See *wet trapping*.

keepaway   When creating a trapping solution for images reversed-out to white from a complex color, a keepaway is used. Typically this involves reversing type out of a multi-color black (also called *rich black)*. The second and third colors are choked, or kept away from the white edge, while the black ink is used to define the final outline. The result is a clean white image with little chance of an individual color peeking out from behind the black if the press goes out of register. Also known as *hold back.*

keylines   See *mechanicals*

kiss-fit   See *butt-fit.*

knockout   A hole left in an object to accommodate the printing of another object or color. The concept of knockout is that which creates the need for trapping objects for printing on PostScript imagesetters. Every object in PostScript, by default, is an opaque object. Thus if one object prints on top of another, it will leave a knockout of itself in the lower object. We create traps—tiny overlapping perimeters—around these knockouts to create a properly trapped job. See also *overprint.*

lap register   A synonym for trapping, referring to the overlapping of colors to create register traps. See also *trapping.*

lines-per-inch   Lines per inch is the measurement most often used to describe the frequency of dots in halftone images. The root of this unit of measure is the *ruling* of glass halftone screens used decades ago in making halftones on metal plates, and later, on film. Lines-per-inch values measure potential halftone dots in a *linear* inch. Typical values are 85 for newsprint, 133 for web offset printing, 150-175 for commercial printing, and higher for specialty printing processes. The many measurements of units-per-inch in the electronic graphic arts industry are very confusing and commonly misused and misunderstood. See also *dots-per-inch* and *pixels-per-inch.*

loose register   A printing term describing a job that requires no close positioning of colors. Often designers create jobs with loose register to save money in prepress. Since colors usually don't need trapping in this type of printing, the cost of preparing the film for plates is much lower.

mechanicals   Artwork prepared for printing. Mechanicals are the photomechanical part of the reproduction process. Also called *art boards, keylines,* or *paste ups.*

misregisteration   When two colors in a printed piece go out of position relative to one another on the printing press, which trapping can overcome to a degree.

moiré   A pattern of interference created by screens that are too close in frequency and angle to one another, yet not exactly the same. Moiré is such a serious problem in printing that years of work have been devoted to its elimination or reduction. Halftone color separations are angled at discrete angles to reduce the tendency to form moiré patterns.

natural trap   A trap made of common colors, where each of the intersecting colors contains at least a percentage of the other color.

overprint   A term used to describe the act of printing one color of ink on top of another. Black is commonly printed on top of other colors for text. Though it is possible to overprint any color over any other, new colors are created by the technique, and these colors may not have been intended by the designer. PostScript never overprints colors at default settings; overprinting must be done consciously by the person preparing the design for output. Also known as *surprint.*

paste-ups   The artwork prepared on art boards for printing. Paste-ups usually include corner and trim marks, photographic position information and ID numbers of names, type and line illustrations, and color-break overlays. Paste-ups are photographed in a process camera before they can be used for printing. Also known as *mechanicals* or *art boards.*

phantom trap   See *spread.*

pixel   A word derived from picture element, the pixel is the smallest unit of image that can be drawn by a computer monitor. The pixel is also the unit of measure for computer bitmap files, whose resolution is measured in pixels-per-inch or pixels per centimeter. See also *bitmap* and *raster.*

pixels-per-inch (ppi)   Once an image is scanned into a computer system, its resolution (in dpi, or *dots-per-inch*) can be expressed as a value of pixels in a linear inch. The relationship of pixels to final halftone dots can be modified in software, making the file larger or smaller in final output. See also *lines-per-inch* and *dots-per-inch*.

PostScript   A page description language developed by Adobe Systems, Inc. PostScript uses a system of Cartesian coordinates to position and print any kind of image—photographic, illustrative, or typographic. PostScript is both a programming language and a method by which images are drawn on film or paper by a laser imagesetter. PostScript is resident in most photographic imagesetters and desktop laser printers.

progressive trap   Another technique for keepaway trapping where different colors are kept-away from the detail-holding color by different amounts.

raster   An image presented in pixel or bitmapped format. All images created for output on a PostScript imagesetter are converted on output to rasterized information that is drawn to film or paper by a modulated laser beam.

rasterize   The process of converting all of the graphic information in a page from vectors, typographic characters, and photo files into instructions for the imagesetter. These instructions come in two types: laser on/laser off (x-axis), and advance material (y-axis). On most drum-based imagesetters the laser beam is moved rather than the material.

register   The correct positioning of colors of ink on a printed sheet. If colors are printed in perfect position, they are said to be in-register. Misregistration, or out-of-register printing is corrected by trapping. See also *hairline register, loose register,* and *lap register.*

rich black   A black composed of solid black (K) plus lesser amounts of the other process colors. A rich black typically consists of 100% K and at least 30% yellow (Y), magenta (M), and cyan (C). In spot color printing, rich blacks contain a similar percentage of the spot colors. Sometimes just one reinforcing color is used, for example 40% cyan under black.

RIP   **R**aster **I**mage **P**rocessors accept information from the designer's computer and convert the information into rasterized (bitmapped) files of information that are printed on an imagesetter. RIPs usually contain a complex circuit board, a hard disk for type font and temporary job storage, and a controller board that understands the incoming PostScript file, and which speaks the control language of the laser film recorder that actually images the photographic material.

screen angle   When printing color separations, the halftone screens of the individual color must be aligned to unique angles in order to prevent (or at least reduce) the formation of interference called moiré patterns. The industry standard screen angles are: C: 105° M: 75° Y: 90° K: 45°. Many variations exist, as do minute modifications of these to produce interference-free halftones on PostScript imagesetters. Don't be alarmed if you see an ID line printed on a separation for magenta indicating an angle of 161.613° This translates into an Adobe Accurate Screen angle of 91.613° off the normal angle; you can ignore the 90° component as a mathematical deviation. The remaining 1.613 degrees is the correction for moiré prevention.

service bureau   Businesses that image computer files onto film or paper for clients. In the design and prepress industries these service bureaus normally operate PostScript imagesetters.

sheet-fed press   A printing press that receives paper in single sheets taken from a stack of paper. These presses usually deliver excellent quality due to their ability to hold and print the material with great precision. Typical sheet-fed presses are 25 to 40 inches in width, and print from 6,000 to 10,000 impressions per hour. The sheet-fed press is commonly used for general commercial printing for press runs of up to 100,000 impressions. Longer runs usually call for web printing where the images are printed on a continuous roll of paper and cut into sheets after printing.

shrink   See *choke*.

skinny   See *choke*.

spread   The opposite of *choke*, these are duplicate films made in a contact frame with a sandwich of clear film in between. Overexposure of the duplicate negative film through a diffusion sheet causes the resulting image to grow in size relative to the original. The spread, in combination with an unmodified second color, will create a trapped image. Also known as *fatty, phantom trap,* or *swell.*

squeeze   See *choke.*

stripping   The process of combining photographic images onto carrier sheets for correct page positioning, photo placement, and proper register. Image assembly is also called *stripping,* a process that originally involved removing the emulsion of a photographic image and transferring it to another photographic carrier. The term *image assembly* is preferred in the printing industry today, because stripper has another—more graphic—meaning.

surprint   See *overprint.*

swell   See *spread.*

trapping   The intentional overlapping of colors along common boundaries to prevent unprinted paper from showing in the event of misregistration in printing. Also called *color trapping, choke-and-spread, fatties-and-skinnies, lap register, grips,* and *shrink-and-spread.* Not to be confused with *wet trapping.*

variable width trapping   Trapping set at different widths, depending on the colors involved. This might be especially useful where complementary colors overlap. For example, traps around a green object on a blue background might be wider than traps around a yellow background, because the yellow traps could be more obvious. Variable width trapping is particularly useful at the intersection of gradations where blends are complex. Some systems allow for variable trapping; others force all traps in one page to the same width.

vector   Illustrations created on a computer with vector software use mathematical descriptions, rather than rows of computer pixels, to describe their elements. Vector programs usually follow the scheme of Cartesian coordinates for positioning, and a measurement unit for distances traveled. A vector program would draw a line by a set of instructions like these: .5 setlinewidth 120 312 moveto 516 719 lineto drawline.

web press   A printing press that prints on continuous rolls of paper or other substrate. Large runs are usually relegated to web presses. Newspapers, packaging, labels, and most magazines are printed on web presses. Modern web presses are capable of matching the quality of sheet-fed presses with no difficulty, at a tremendous rate of speed.

wet trapping   When wet ink is printed on wet ink, as on most sheet-fed and web-fed offset presses, a concern of the printer is that the inks adhere to the inks already printed. Also, wet-trapped ink can cause a color shift in the printed image as a result of the interaction of the multiple layers of ink. The formulation of inks is modified according to the order in which the ink will be printed, the tack of the ink adjusted to fit the needs of the press operator.

This term is unrelated to the intentional overlapping of colors to avoid misregistration in printing, or color trapping, which is the subject of this book.

Index

A

absolute registers, 11
abutting (colors), 10
Adobe Illustrator, 57,
    104, 113
    blends, 109
    color, 107
    PageMaker, 65
    Photoshop
        (rasterizing), 67
    QuarkXPress, 65
Adobe PageMaker, 64, 117
    Create Keyline, 118
    FreeHand, 65
    Illustrator, 65
    TrapMaker, 117
Adobe Photoshop, 66
    automatic trapping, 116
    CMYK images, 66
    rasterizing, 67
Adobe TrapWise, 77
air conditioning, 35
algorithms (software), 47
amount (trapping), 18
Apple Color Picker, 22
automatic trapping
    Photoshop, 116
    QuarkXPress, 121

B

backgrounds
    (FreeHand), 111
bitmaps (QuarkXPress), 124
black
    overprinting, 41, 103
    QuarkXPress, 123
blends
    FreeHand, 109
    Illustrator, 109
bounce (misregistration), 29

C

CEPS (color electronic
    prepress systems), 68
chart (workflow), 96
chokes, 14-16, 101
    QuarkXPress, 124
CMYK images, 66
color
    abutting, 10
    CMYK images, 66
    common, 42
    comparing, 22
    darkness, 100
    dominate-subordinate
        relationships, 21
    FreeHand, 107
    grayscale, 21
    Illustrator, 107
    knockout, 11
    lightness, 100
    overprinting, 39
    percentages, 42
    presses, single color
        printing multi-
        color, 30
    process, 24
    pure, 22
    QuarkXPress, 123
    reversing-out, 63
    secondary, 22
    spot printing, 24
color electronic prepress
    systems (CEPS), 68
color wheel, 21-22
common colors, 42
comparing colors, 22
composite images, 50
CorelDRAW!, 59
Create Keyline
    (PageMaker), 118

D

Dalim Trapping System, 84
darkness (color), 102
dedicated trapping
    software, 125
designers, 89
    prepress, 91
diffusion, 17
display type, 48
dominate-subordinate
    relationships (color), 21
dry wetting, 9
duplicating film, 16

E

environmental controls, 35
EPS files, 101
    QuarkXPress, 124
errors
    misregistration, 28
    platemaking, 33
exposures
    diffusion, 17
    film, 16
    vacuum exposure
        frames, 32

F

files (EPS), 101
film
    choking, 14
    duplicating
        exposures, 16
    exposures, 16
    light integrators, 32
    misregistration, 31
    spreads, 14

flexographic printing, 53
FreeHand, 59, 104
    backgrounds, 111
    blends, 109
    color, 107
    outlines, 110
    PageMaker, 65
    QuarkXPress, 65
    strokes, 109

G

GATF (Graphics Art
   Technical Foundation), 10
gradations, 50-52
grayscale, 21
grips, 9

H

hairline registers (color), 10
heating (environmental
   controls), 35
hold backs (negative
   spaces), 60
human error
    misregistration, 31
    platemaking, 33
humidity control, 35

I

Illustrator, 57, 104, 113
    blends, 109
    color, 107
    PageMaker, 65
    Photoshop
     (rasterizing), 67
    QuarkXPress, 65
images (composite), 50

imagesetters
    misregistration, 90
    Rampage RIPs, 81
    Scitex Dolev, 80
inks (wet trapping), 9
IslandTrapper, 74

K-L

keepaways (negative
   spaces), 60
knockout colors, 11

lap registers, 10
large type, 48
leakage (negative spaces), 60
light integrators, 32
lightness (color), 100
lithography
    chokes, 14
    spreads, 14
    standards, 20
loose registers, 10

M

Macromedia FreeHand, 59
misregistration, 28
    bounce, 29
    film, 31
    human errror, 31
    imagesetters, 90
    paper
      composition, 29
      stress, 29
    press wear, 30
    printing, multi-color on
     single color press, 30
    stripping materials, 31
multi-color presses, 30

N

negative spaces
    hold backs, 60
    keepaways, 60
    leakage, 60
newspaper presses, 19

O

objects (QuarkXPress), 122
outlines (FreeHand), 110
overprinting, 39
    black, 41, 103
    parsing, 41
    PostScript separation
     programs, 41
    strokes, 108
    type, 48

P

PageMaker, 64, 117
    Create Keyline, 118
    FreeHand, 65
    Illustrator, 65
    TrapMaker, 117
paper
    composition, 29
    manufacturing, 29
    misregistration
     composition, 29
     stress, 29
    printing stress, 29
parsing (overprinting), 41
percentages (color), 42
photographs, 49
Photoshop, 66
    automatic trapping, 116
    CMYK images, 66
    rasterizing, 67

platemaking, 33
PostScript separation
  programs, 41
PostScript trapping
  Adobe TrapWise, 77
  Dalim Trapping
    System, 84
  IslandTrapper, 74
  proofreading, 82
  Rampage RIPs, 81
  Scitex Dolev imageset-
    ters, 80
prepress
  CEPS (color electronic
    prepress systems), 68
  Dalim Trapping
    System, 84
  designers, 91
prepress services, 38
presses
  environmental
    controls, 35
  misregistration, 30
  newspapers, 19
  printing multi-color on
    single color, 30
  sheet-fed, 19
printers
  misregistration, 90
  trapping, 38
printing
  flexographic, 53
  gradations, 50
  multi-color on single
    color
    presses, 30
  overprinting, 39
    black, 103
  spot color, 24
  standards, 20
process colors, 24

proofreading, 102
  Postscript trapping, 82
pure color, 22

Q

QuarkXPress, 64, 119
  automatic trapping, 121
  bitmaps, 124
  chokes, 124
  color, 123
  EPS files, 124
  FreeHand, 65
  Illustrator, 65
  objects, 122
  SXetchPad, 124
  text, 124

R

Rampage RIPs 81
rasterizing (Photoshop), 67
registers, 10
  absolute, 11
  hairline, 10
  lap, 10
  loose, 10
  tight, 10
reverses (negative spaces), 60
reversing-out colors, 63

S

Scitex Dolev imagesetters, 80
screen tints, 23
secondary color, 22
sheet-fed presses, 19
single color presses, 30
small type, 46

software
  Adobe Illustrator, 57,
    104, 113
    blends, 109
    color, 107
    PageMaker, 65
    Photoshop (raster-
      izing), 67
    QuarkXPress, 65
  Adobe PageMaker,
    64, 117
    Create Keyline, 118
    FreeHand, 65
    Illustrator, 65
    TrapMaker, 117
  Adobe Photoshop, 66
    automatic
      trapping, 116
    CMYK images, 66
    rasterizing, 67
  Adobe TrapWise, 77
  algorithms, 47
  CorelDRAW!, 59
  dedicated trapping
    programs, 125
  EPS files, 101
  FreeHand, 104
  Illustrator, 104, 113
  IslandTrapper, 74
  Macromedia
    FreeHand, 59
  PageMaker, 117
  QuarkXPress, 64, 119
    automatic
      trapping, 121
    bitmaps, 124
    chokes, 124
    color, 123
    EPS files, 124
    FreeHand, 65
    Illustrator, 65

objects, 122
    SXetchPad, 124
    text, 124
Rampage RIPs, 81
spot color (printing), 24
spreads, 14, 16, 101
standards (lithography), 20
stripping
    (misregistration), 31
strokes, 108
    FreeHand, 109
SXetchPad
    (QuarkXPress), 124

type
    display, 48
    overprinting, 48
    QuarkXPress, 124
    small, 46

V-Z

vacuum exposure frames, 32

wet trapping, 9
workflow chart, 98

T

text
    display type, 48
    overprinting, 48
    QuarkXPress, 124
    small type, 46
    trapping, 21
tight registers, 10
time considerations, 88
tints (screen), 23
TrapMaker, 117
trapping, 8
    amount, 18
    dry, 9
    printers, 38
    screen tints, 23
    text, 21
    wet, 9
TrapWise, 77

PLUG YOURSELF INTO...

THE MACMILLAN INFORMATION SUPERLIBRARY™

Free information and vast computer resources from the world's leading computer book publisher—online!

FIND THE BOOKS THAT ARE RIGHT FOR YOU!

A complete online catalog, plus sample chapters and tables of contents give you an in-depth look at *all* of our books, including hard-to-find titles. It's the best way to find the books you need!

- STAY INFORMED with the latest computer industry news through our online newsletter, press releases, and customized Information SuperLibrary Reports.

- GET FAST ANSWERS to your questions about MCP books and software.

- VISIT our online bookstore for the latest information and editions!

- COMMUNICATE with our expert authors through e-mail and conferences.

- DOWNLOAD SOFTWARE from the immense MCP library:
  - Source code and files from MCP books
  - The best shareware, freeware, and demos

- DISCOVER HOT SPOTS on other parts of the Internet.

- WIN BOOKS in ongoing contests and giveaways!

TO PLUG INTO MCP: ➤ WORLD WIDE WEB: **http://www.mcp.com**

GOPHER: gopher.mcp.com

FTP: ftp.mcp.com

The Complete Guide to Trapping, Second Edition

Hayden
Books

Online Information
MacTCP Account

Addressing Style (Manually, Server, Dynamically): _____

IP Address (if Manually addressed): _____

Gateway Address (if Manually addressed): _____

Network Class (if Manually addressed and necessary): _____

Subnet Mask (if Manually addressed and necessary): _____

Domain Name Server (default): _____

Domain Name Server (backup): _____

SMTP Server: _____

NNTP Server: _____

POP Account: _____

Email Address: _____

Connection Type (PPP, SLIP, ARA, Network): _____

Phone Number: _____

Port Speed: _____

Modem Init String: _____

Shell Accounts

Unix Host #1: _____ _____ _____ _____
phone number/speed   userid   password   modem init string

_____
notes

Unix Host #2: _____ _____ _____ _____
phone number/speed   userid   password   modem init string

_____
notes

Bulletin Board Accounts

BBS #1: _____ _____ _____ _____
phone number/speed   userid   password   modem init string

_____
notes

BBS #2: _____ _____ _____ _____
phone number/speed   userid   password   modem init string

_____
notes

UUCP Account

Host: _____ _____ _____ _____
phone number/speed   userid   password   modem init string

_____ _____ _____
mail server name   news server name   Administrator's email address

_____
notes

Note: Storing your passwords here could be a security breach. Only do so if you are sure this won't be a problem.

The Complete Guide to Trapping, Second Edition

Hayden
Books

Online Information

Commercial Online Services

America Online: _____ _____ _____ _____
                phone number/speed   userid   password   modem init string

                notes

AppleLink: _____ _____ _____ _____
                phone number/speed   userid   password   modem init string

                notes

BIX: _____ _____ _____ _____
                phone number/speed   userid   password   modem init string

                notes

CompuServe: _____ _____ _____ _____
                phone number/speed   userid   password   modem init string

                notes

Delphi: _____ _____ _____ _____
                phone number/speed   userid   password   modem init string

                notes

eWorld: _____ _____ _____ _____
                phone number/speed   userid   password   modem init string

                notes

GEnie: _____ _____ _____ _____
                phone number/speed   userid   password   modem init string

                notes

MCI Mail: _____ _____ _____ _____
                phone number/speed   userid   password   modem init string

                notes

Outland: _____ _____ _____ _____
                phone number/speed   userid   password   modem init string

                notes

Prodigy: _____ _____ _____ _____
                phone number/speed   userid   password   modem init string

                notes

Note: Storing your passwords here could be a security breach. Only do so if you are sure this won't be a problem.

design

solutions

from hayden books

 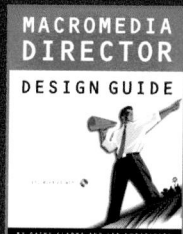  

Photoshop Type Magic
Highlights more than 40 different type effects, including airbrushed, beveled, blurred, chiseled, graffiti, neon, rubber stamped, embossed, and more.
ISBN: 1-56830-220-7, $30.00 USA
256 pp., 6 7/8 x 9, New - Casual - Accomplished - Expert
Covers All Platforms

Macromedia Director Design Guide
An all-in-one user's guide to composing brilliant, sophisticated interactive multimedia!
ISBN: 1-56830-062-X, $29.95 USA
198 pp., 6 7/8 x 9, New - Casual - Accomplished - Expert
Covers Through Version 4 for Macintosh

Designer's Guide to the Internet
Written by a prominent writer, educator, and graphic designer, Mike Zender, this is a useful resource for computer-literate—but Internet shy—designers.
ISBN: 1-56830-229-0, $30.00 USA
350 pp., 7 3/8 x 9 1/8, Accomplished - Expert
Covers designing for on-line services, marketing, research and business uses, costs, ethics, software and file formats

Adobe Illustrator Creative Techniques
This quick reference covers the 150 most common Illustrator tasks, from drawing techniques to text manipulation and color use.
ISBN: 1-56830-133-2, $35.00 USA
320 pp., 8 1/2 x 11, Casual - Accomplished
Covers Version 5.5 for Macintosh

Available at your local fine bookstore or wherever communication arts are sold.
Or call 1-800-763-7438 and mention the source code: 1-56830-098-0

About the Disk

By opening this package, you are agreeing to be bound by the following agreement:

This software product is copyrighted, and all rights are reserved by the publisher and author. You are licensed to use this software on a single computer. You may copy and/or modify the software as needed to facilitate your use of it on a single computer. Making copies of the software for any other purpose is a violation of the United States copyright laws.

This software is sold *as is* without warranty of any kind, either expressed or implied, including but not limited to the implied warranties of merchantability and fitness for a particular purpose. Neither the publisher nor its dealers or distributors assumes any liability for any alleged or actual damages arising from the use of this program. (Some states do not allow for the exclusion of implied warranties, so the exclusion may not apply to you.)